MANUAL FOR RETREAT MASTERS

MANUAL FOR
Retreat Masters

FR. WILLIAM, O.C.D.

THE BRUCE PUBLISHING COMPANY
MILWAUKEE

9573

Imprimi potest:

    FR. CHRISTOPHER LATIMER, O.C.D.

    Provincial

Nihil obstat:

    JOHN A. SCHULIEN

    Censor librorum

Imprimatur:

    ✠ WILLIAM E. COUSINS

    Archbishop of Milwaukee

    April 8, 1960

Library of Congress Catalog Card Number: 60–12649

To the humblest
and most real theologian
I know —
my mother,
Margaret M. McNamara

Preface

Four or five particular things led to the writing of this book:

(1) The Holy See's recent emphasis on pastoral theology.

(2) The astounding growth of the retreat movement.

(3) The relentless pressure exerted on the publishers by many priests requesting that this book be written.

(4) The needs of the layman today, especially the college and high school student, for a living, fresh theology, a personal structure of faith, a Christian humanism.

(5) The author's own almost unbearable responsibility to "get the Gospel to every creature" and to compel all to answer positively, existentially, the most important, pressing question ever asked in the history of the world: "What think ye of Christ?"

FATHER WILLIAM (McNAMARA), O.C.D.

CONTENTS

CONTENTS

PART I

THE RETREAT MASTER

CHAPTER I

The Retreat Master as Spiritual Director

The retreat master is, above all, a spiritual director. He ought, therefore, to have a clear concept of what spiritual direction is and what it involves.

Spiritual direction is "the delegated action of Christ for the edification of His Mystical Body, through the ordinary organ of the priesthood." Of the individual effect of direction, one could say: it is for the formation of the perfect member of the Mystical Body. The fact is that the purpose of spiritual direction is to aid a person to become himself, his best self, a perfect human being; and this is done primarily through a progressive enlightenment of the mind and enlargement of the heart, involving an adequate response to God and other men.

The aim is toward knowledge of God because no one can love what he does not know; and it is impossible really to know God without loving Him, so infinitely attractive is He. "Whoever loves is born of God and knows God; who does not love does not know God for God is love" (I Jn. 4:7). For St. John, then, to know God is not an abstract intellectual process but an experience that involves all of our powers — affective as well as intellectual. And the experience finds concrete manifestation through the exercise of the same affective and knowing faculties in our adjustment to one another. The by-product, the indirect result of the Godward aim of spiritual direction is perfection — the perfection of charity. When a man loves God perfectly, he is perfect.

Spiritual direction is not, therefore, only concerned with moral problems but with the positive concern for the actuation and development of the theological virtues of faith, hope, and charity. And so spiritual direction is not meant to give a precise solution to all moral problems, but to help a person come closer to Christ, the source of his entire spiritual life. Through this personal direction one is led toward the experience of knowing God. Direction does not produce the experience, but it prepares and helps one to achieve, with the grace of God, the necessary disposition for such an experience. And God has given the director a mandate to judge the authenticity of the experience and eventually to help the person manifest this experience in everyday living.

Pope Leo XIII declared it to be "a common law of Providence that souls be led to the loftier spiritual heights by being helped by other men." This is tantamount to saying that spiritual guidance is necessary in order to raise the level of the Christian life in souls, and also to point out that in the hands of God, men, and especially priests, become instruments to produce spiritual growth in souls. "We find at the very origin of the Church a well-known manifestation of this law: although Saul, breathing out threat and carnage, had heard the voice of Christ Himself and had asked Him: Lord, what do You want me to do? he was sent for the answer to Damascus, to Ananias: 'Enter into the city and there it will be told you what you must do'" (*Testem Benevolentiae*).

One needs spiritual direction *in order to begin a spiritual life*. Without it, there is frequently no beginning at all; or if it is begun, it is begun unsteadily, unsurely, from wrong starting points and false principles and unhealthy emphases. It is so important to begin with everything right. It is like getting an airplane off the ground. That is the most important point in the whole flight. The plane is readied; help comes from every direction and source for a successful take-off. Once off the ground and into the air (the plane's proper environment), all is well, ordinarily, and all relax. Something similar is true of the human being in pursuit of the towering objectives of the spiritual life. Once into the supernatural world, into the spirit (a human being's true environment), and led by the Spirit, all is well. But vast and varied help is needed in the beginning. Just as the pilot does, indeed, have general knowledge of aeronautics but needs particular, concrete knowledge *applied* to him and his situation here and now, so the Christian in pursuit of perfection needs at the beginning of his spiritual life a specific, concrete *application* of principles, here and now, in a given situation, with a particular kind of nature, temperament, and disposition. Experienced help is therefore needed. Outside help is necessary for an objective view of self. A man cannot see himself with sure and true objectivity. He cannot see with clarity because of emotional stress, situational pressure, and other debilitating factors. And so he who constitutes himself his own master becomes the disciple of a fool.

Perfection, it is important to remember, has different forms, according to the vast variety of personalities in the world and the particular circumstances and conditions surrounding each one. When this is overlooked by devout but unwise and undirected people, certain unpleasant and unholy things happen. Someone imitates a saint slavishly and stifles the growth of his own unique personality. Another forces himself into a mold and experiences frustration, spoils his humanity. Someone else applies the principles and rules of spiritual growth without imagination or discrimination and so foils his best efforts and thwarts his finest qualities. And so on. The results, in general, are disastrous. To avert them, one does not always need a director, but one does need direction.

Spiritual direction frequently *prevents one from merely*

going through the motions of religion. There are so many
Christians who do not appreciate the magnificent dignity
of their vocation to sanctity, to the perfection of love. There
are so many who have practically no idea of God's immense
love for them, and of the personal nature of that love, and
of the power of that love to do them good, to bring them
indescribable happiness. The seeds of this perfect happiness,
this divine life, are planted in every Christian soul at baptism. But seeds must grow and develop before you reap the
harvest. There are thousands of Christians walking about the
face of the earth bearing in their bodies the Infinite
God of whom they know practically nothing. The majority
in the Church stand on the threshold and go through the
external motions of religion and dutifully profess their faith.
But never have they come to the heart of the Church where
the living God dwells; they do not enjoy their faith, they
do not know God by experience.

The Christian religion has got to come alive in the individual life. A man needs more than abstract knowledge. He
needs to know God firsthand. He needs to go through the
arduous process of loss and gain, trial and error. The supernatural life is necessarily adventurous, dangerous. It is
governed by the principles of sanctity, not safety. One ought
not to risk it alone. And it seems that nobody wants to. And
so they stand on the threshold, fulfilling all their obligations
but missing the joy and the power and the glory of religion.
That is why G. K. Chesterton said: "Christianity has not
been tried and found wanting; it has been found difficult and
left untried." If they would only come all the way in and
drink of the eternal fountain of life bubbling up at the heart
of the Church! But their cry is heard all around the world:
"How can I, unless some man show me."

Without direction it is difficult *to avoid the common
aberrations, inroads, subtle fallacies:* a negative outlook and
approach, the extremes of Pelagianism or Jansenism, pietism,

sentimentalism, fanaticism, or mediocrity; or *to withstand the forces that are against spiritual growth.* Alone, a man cannot ordinarily withstand the constant pressure of human respect, public opinion, the *status quo,* or the pull toward the least common denominator, mass conformity, opportunism, the world, the flesh, and the devil.

As a rule, one needs spiritual direction *for the adequate solving of problems.* Without it, many try to escape problems rather than solve them, which, of course, is spiritually, psychologically, and socially disastrous. With direction it is much easier to solve problems and make decisions and thus grow by one victory after another. It is particularly necessary for assisting a person through the *precarious periods:* transitional stages of prayer, scruples, temptations, doubts, darkness, and crises of all kinds. It is, finally, *an aid to perseverance.* For one aiming at holiness, the most besetting temptation is to give up. He needs periodic checking for stimulation, correction, encouragement; above all, perhaps, for continuity — a continuous thread running straight through all moods, providing orientation and balance to one's whole life, precluding unwholesome periods of elation and depression.

St. Teresa undertook nothing without direction. She says: "Every Christian should try to consult some learned person if he can, and the more learned the person the better. Those who walk in the way of prayer have the greater need of learning; and the more spiritual they are, the greater is their need. . . . I, myself, through not knowing what to do, have suffered much and lost a great deal of time."

Lack of spiritual growth is accredited by St. John of the Cross to the absence of spiritual direction; "because they do not understand themselves and lack competent and alert directors who will guide them to the summit." This is not God's fault, as the saint goes on to point out. "When God says or reveals something to a soul, he gives this same soul to whom He says it, a kind of inclination to tell it to the person to whom it is fitting it should be told. Until this has been done, there is not entire satisfaction because the man has not been reassured by another man like himself." A layman who takes seriously the command to be perfect needs spiritual direction even more than a religious.

St. Paul went to the Apostles to be confirmed in his faith. St. Peter, although taught and favored by God Himself, went astray on his own with regard to a ceremony concerning the Gentiles. The Fathers of the desert, despite an insatiable thirst for solitude, gathered together for the sake of direction. The majority of saints had spiritual directors, and all of them had some kind of direction. With some, the relationship between director and directed led to a warm-hearted, holy friendship in which both found, besides light for their ascent of the mount of perfection, a marvelous spiritual enrichment and fruitfulness in works of mercy.

Holiness is most desirable in a director. It is what makes him like God. He is God-centered, Christ-conscious. Although he is so useful and available to all who seek or need him, he is wholly other; he is charitable, humble, and prayerful, a collaborator of God. Holiness alone has respect for the absolute right of God over the soul. A holy director will regard himself merely as an instrument that acts from the outside. He will regard every person as sacred. Each soul is created immediately by God without intermediary; it is consequently ordained immediately to Him, and there can be no one between it and God. The director can only intervene from without, striving to give to people confided to him the most suitable means to advance in the way of sanctity; but it is God who leads them. "Only God can deify," said St. Thomas. Consequently, a director is only a servant, a servant of souls, a servant of the Holy Spirit in souls. The director's attitude ought to be that of John the Baptist: "He must increase and I must decrease."

The holy director will stand with immense, awful fear and reverence before the mystery of a human person and before the even more wonderful mystery of God in a human life. He will not rush in where angels fear to tread. St. John of the Cross has severe words for spiritual guides who, he says, "like rough blacksmiths know only the use of the hammer," and bids them remember that "here the Holy Spirit is the principal agent and the real guide of souls, who never ceases to take care of them and never neglects any means by which they may profit and draw near to God quickly and in the surest way." This is a delicate business, and no task for hardheaded, coldhearted people at all. The whole purpose of all human instrumentality is to lead the soul to that degree of sanctity where it is totally docile to the ultimate Director, who alone is holy, the Holy Spirit.

The holy director will be keenly aware of how unique each person is. St. John of the Cross exclaims: "Hardly could we find one that even half resembles another." All are fed by the same bread of life — but! The director must regard this mystery with respect. The action of grace in the soul will reveal to him the divine name by which it is called.

I once lived near a mansion where only one of the many gardeners employed there had succeeded with every one of the roses. I asked him the secret of his success. He told me that the other gardeners treated all the roses not unwisely, but too generally — they treated them all in precisely the same way; whereas he himself watched across the months each rosebush separately, and followed out for each plant, that plant's special *attrait* as to soil, manure, sun, air, water, support, shelter, and the like.

The spiritual director needs to treat each person as separately, distinctly, and carefully as that. Immeasurable damage has been done by directors who have advised or governed with a sameness, a coldness, a generality that kills creativity and originality; who have imposed upon their charges lifeless systems and humorless programs that are outworn, incompatible, unsound, and most undesirable; and who have, therefore, robbed from the people they directed or governed the very foundation for any kind of greatness or nobility — *the spontaneous zest for life.*

The poignant lament of our late Holy Father Pius XII that "man is being despoiled of his personality" is not merely for the enemies of the Faith. It is for all those, busy with endless classifications of good and bad, for those who think they know everything about their brothers and sisters in religion, their subjects, their fellow workers, their employees, who don't respect sufficiently God's mysteries in dealing with souls. This is the most subtle form of that desolating scandal that so horrified our Lord. Better to be bound and cast into the sea than be the source of this kind of direction.

It is a great privilege of the holy director to contemplate at times the work of God in souls, and to collaborate discreetly — always in the shadow — so that the power, mercy, and wisdom of God, admirable in all His works but especially in His saints, may shine forth and be glorified.

Without prudence, a director would do more harm than good. It must be real prudence, though, the positive, dynamic, manly virtue with a rich, broad sweep of intelligence. One must never confuse this virtue with spineless caution. It is anything but that. Prudence chooses not always the safest means to the end, but the best and most appropriate here and now. The director must be bold, daring, decisive; and at the same time exquisitely delicate. He is confronted continually by the darkness of the divine and the complexity of human nature. He must cope with the demands of God and human weakness. He will need to expend all of his spiritual might and wit toward discerning God's will. Rashness and hastiness are always perilous. So are complacency in one's own judgment, perfunctory observations, unwillingness to admit a mistake or to change one's mind, to reverse a decision. Though He must not be crippled by hesitation or undue delay, he must be prepared to wait. The great doers are often the most patient, watchful men. He must attune the soul to God's pace, God's goal, in His manner. And so he must be awake, alert, responsive. He must not only think and pray. He must seek counsel, study, sweat, labor, worry, and above all, love. Without the driving force of love, the intuitive power of love, his direction will be desultory, weak, superficial, blind. Love is an irrevocable commitment to another person, a donation, a surrender — without sentimentality or softness. He who makes decisions outside of this context is a coward, and thus completely unsuitable for representing, either as a director or a superior, a God who is Love.

It is impossible to overestimate the value of experience in a director. All the masters of the spiritual life have spoken from their own experience or from that of souls they had been able to observe closely. Techniques and methods cannot track down the action of God in a soul; they may even hinder His action and restrict it. Without experience a director can be a kind and passive witness, but it does not seem that he can, without supernatural enlightenment, encourage and direct with authority as his function obliges him. Even the signs of contemplation of St. John of the Cross need to be experienced in some degree before judicious application can be made to concrete cases.

We know how indebted St. Teresa of Avila was to experienced directors: St. Francis Borgia, St. Peter of Alcantara. She says: "I have come across souls so constrained and afflicted because of the inexperience of their director that I have been really sorry for them."

An inexperienced director may easily thwart once and for all the soaring spirit of the soul, either through lack of understanding or timidity; or again by letting it exhaust itself prematurely by excessive mortifications, not having had experience of their rigor or their effects. And so there is no substitute for experience. Most tragic mistakes of direction are made by young and ardent, but inexperienced, men.

A thorough grasp of the basic principles of ascetic and mystical theology is indispensable to anyone who wishes to give enlightened help to others in pursuit of perfection. He must not be so captivated by or absorbed in one branch of theology or one aspect of the spiritual life as to lose his balanced perspective of the whole; for instance, a liturgist who knows nothing of contemplation, or a contemplative who ignores the liturgy. He must possess a unifying synthesis of all theological science. There are no partitions among dogmatic, moral, ascetic, and mystical theology. There is a science of God and His dealings with men, branching out in different ways but always demanding a fixed center.

St. Teresa had a real penchant for learned men, especially as directors. She preferred them even to pious men. "The more learned the better," she said. And not just ordinary learning; she had no use for those pseudo intellectuals who couldn't explain the manner of God's presence in the soul. She speaks of "timid, half-learned men whose shortcomings have cost me very dear."

It is not enough to know theology. A director must also know psychology, that science which opens up the mysterious realm of the subconscious. St. John of the Cross is the great psychologist of the spiritual life. He should be read and reread. Modern psychology has made an enormous contribution toward the understanding of the whole man, the discovery of the causes of mental illness, the remedial treatment and rehabilitation of the mentally ill, and above all, perhaps, the positive principles of mental hygiene, the way to become a full-grown, mature, integrated man. All this ought to be known and utilized by the director.

But in this field of psychology especially, "a little knowledge is a dangerous thing." Even full knowledge is dangerous, since the science itself is still very young, weak, and unsure of itself. Unfortunately, there is very much we do not know. In fact, we seem to be in ignorance of the more important things. The miasma of ignorance which surrounds the topic of psychology, and the consequent Vesuvius of ceaseless chatter about complexes, repressions, inhibitions, childhood traumas, anxieties, frustrations, and Oedipus yearnings have had a most confusing, debilitating effect upon thoughtful adults. The educational system itself has been unfavorably, detrimentally psychiatrized.

All this is not to say that our knowledge of psychical processes and phenomena is deficient in quantity or trivial in quality; but it does lack the finality, completeness, and authority that many directors and superiors are attributing to it. The best psychologists and psychoanalysts assure us that most of the theories we hold today in the areas of motivation, emotions, and personality will look "corny" fifty years hence. It would be folly, then, for a director to adhere too rigidly and too devotedly to contemporary psychological theories, just as it is unreasonable for superiors to use the interpreted data by psychological tests as the major factor in the judgment of vocations.

It has been suggested by Dr. J. A. Gengereili in *The Saturday Review* that a ten year moratorium be invoked in public pronunciamentos by all "personality experts." He concludes: "a protracted and restful silence in the mass-communication networks regarding the mind and personality would do much toward tranquilizing the Age of Anxiety."

This may seem an unnecessary concentration on the retreat master as spiritual director. After all, he may never meet these particular retreatants again in a lifetime. It doesn't matter. If the priest is what a director ought to be, perhaps a single encounter with him in the ideal atmosphere of a retreat will be enough to engender a permanent, Godward orientation. Very often, however, a priest either as retreat master, chaplain, or confessor, will speak periodically to the same group. This is "group direction" and, invariably, it involves a great deal of personal direction.

At any rate, during the retreat the priest must be available whenever possible for confession and personal, individual meetings with the retreatants. This time spent with retreatants between conferences is usually more important and fruitful than the conferences themselves. This may be the first time that the retreatant has taken religion or Christ or his own vocation seriously. This time of grace must not be wasted. The deep, most real aspects of life are stripped of church-school formality and artificiality and take on flesh and blood. This may be the single instance when a person dares — or finds it convenient — to discuss a problem, or confess a certain sin.

In three days' time the priest utterly exhausts himself in trying to reach as many of his retreatants as possible. By words and actions he must so radiate the kindness, sympathy, and understanding of Christ that all who are anxious, confused, upset, restless, searching, discouraged will be inclined to tell everything and anything, especially in the sacred tribunal of penance. Such is the high point of a retreat, particularly a high school retreat.

CHAPTER II

The Retreat Master for Teen-Agers

The retreat master is pre-eminently a spiritual director, not a preacher. In other words, the thing of paramount importance in a teen-age retreat is not the conference that leaves the audience breathless or tearful but the deep, abiding communication of divine truth that gives direction to their lives.

The teen-ager's desire and need for spiritual direction is one of the most obvious things in the world today. This desire and need has been expressed persistently, pleadingly, over a rather long period of time. It can no longer be ignored. It is imperative that all priests respond with zeal, intelligence, and untiring labor.

So many young people are restless and have not found anything of the world sufficiently engaging, absorbing, or satisfying. So many have become aware of their apostolic responsibility and are at the same time conscious of their spiritual poverty. They are hungry for the things of God; they are crying out for bread and they must not be handed a stone in the form of a weak or inadequate excuse such as: "too advanced for me," "no time," "not necessary," "big crowds at confession," "better to be just an ordinary Christian." Now is the hour. We must meet their demands if they are to remain effective instruments of Christ's peace and power in the world. God has called them all to divine union; the Church has called them all to work — the most divine work; it is the duty of priests to help them in every way possible to achieve their vocation.

This is what the teen-agers are asking for. The consistent response of the majority to personal inquiries and questionnaires has been a plea for real spiritual direction: "Please give us a spiritual retreat." "Don't give us a negative retreat." "Tell us how to pray." "Speak on the love of God." "Please don't treat us like children or criminals." "Please don't concentrate on sex." "We want something different, something deeper, something positive."

These are typical of the vast majority of requests that high school students make to retreat masters. There are, of course, a few who want nothing but talks on sex; there are some who simply want to be entertained; and there are others who want no part of the retreat at all. All of these must be considered, coped with, and appealed to. But the majority must not be left uninspired, unchallenged, without direction.

For three days the retreat master will be completely absorbed with all of them — some eager, some listless, some defiant. He will be overwhelmed with the fearful conviction that their whole future, for time and eternity, may well depend on how they accept or resist God's grace in this retreat. The immense and incalculable sanctity of some will leave him momentarily breathless. The hardened, sinful attitude of others will be, at times, frustrating. And between these extremes there will be the legions of the indifferent, apparently untouched by Catholic education, who will make up tomorrow's tremendous leakage from the Church.

This is no small challenge for the retreat master. These people are smarter, more serious, restless, and inventive than ever before. Their flair for independence, their readiness to follow a leader, their spirit of daring, their search for anything new — what fertile natural soil to develop basic wrong attitudes for the future! If even one of them can be reached now, and directed, the lives of thousands may be affected in the future. In God's providence, the salvation of children yet unborn will depend on resolutions and decisions made on *this* high school retreat. It is, and ought to be, a frightening experience.

Most retreat masters find that teen-age retreats are the hardest and yet the most enjoyable. No ordinary talks will do. These people need to be won, convinced, moved. This is a tall order, achieved not by oratory or a beautiful style but only by the grace of God that works through the intense, infectious enthusiasm, the irresistible sincerity, and the blunt, hammering blows of a direct approach that fairly sweeps them off their feet. They must not think this is part of school, an educational program, or just another sermon. They must sense and feel and know with a deep inner conviction that "what Father is talking about must be awfully important, very real; nothing vague, sentimental, pietistic. By the tone in his voice, the expression in his face, the examples he gives — I can see that it is important for me *personally*."

There must be, always, concrete, practical applications of doctrine to *them*. If your topic does not mean anything to them and their daily lives, they are bored — and you will know it. You may by your innate power of eloquence and charm capture and engage them during retreat. But will such a shallow, flimsy impression endure? By their fruits you will know them.

Teen-agers are very demanding. They want a retreat master who is priestly but not aloof, dignified but not cold, warmhearted but not sentimental, frank but not uncouth, humorous but never vulgar, lighthearted but never silly. And their demands are just.

All does not depend on the retreat master alone. The tone, spirit, and success of the high school retreat depends largely upon the kind of preparation carried on by the students under the direction of the faculty and chaplain long before the retreat actually begins.* Such a preparation makes all the difference in the world. With it, the retreat becomes

* See Appendix 1 for practical helps on this matter.

the major spiritual event of the year. The students look forward to it with heightened anticipation, they vie with one another toward its perfect fulfillment, they remember each annual retreat fondly, distinctly, and can discuss this retreat intelligently, fruitfully; and their families and acquaintances have seen the good effects in their lives.

High school retreats that are so well prepared are often superior even to many "closed retreats." Hence it is hard to understand why so many Catholic high schools still have no annual retreat. To limit this privilege to seniors is a mistake. Sad to say, it is often too late when they are seniors. It is a good idea to have four retreats — one for each year separately. To have one for all four years together is certainly better than none at all.

The retreat program is also a determining factor of a good retreat. Too many conferences, for instance, that squeeze out precious time for thought, prayer, reading, private meetings with the retreat master, are harmful. Conferences that are too long (a half hour should be the maximum length) are equally injurious. A multiplicity of devotions and exercises "to keep them busy" is unnecessary if there has been adequate preparation. It is certainly undesirable.

Silence is indispensable. And so is solitude, if at all possible — times and places to be *alone* with God. A very rich, properly executed liturgy, with active, intelligent participation should be one of the absolute requirements and outstanding features of the retreat.

The value of the question box is dubious. It is frequently an element of distraction and disturbance in retreat. The same questions are asked in every retreat. They can be anticipated by including the pertinent information in the ordinary conference matter. A discussion period is ordinarily of much greater value — particularly on the last day when things begin to bog down.

CHAPTER III

Retreat Material in General

The retreat master must so understand modern men and women, particularly teen-agers, that he knows just what to talk about. Guesswork will not do. Neither will his own bent or his own convenience — giving whatever "flows out" of him, or what he "happens to have on hand." There's too much at stake. Three days is such a short time that one must be most selective and discriminating in choice of subject matter, ruthlessly discarding any and all topics that are not *best* for them here and now. Choosing the material is one task. Another, a more Herculean task that will test the patience, zeal, and theological training of the priest, is to aim this matter straight at the problem of modern living, tying it up with the hopes and designs of the Retreatants.

The retreat master's aim is that of all good high school teachers: to give them a handful of big, basic ideas; if they hold on to these ideas and LIVE them the rest of their lives, then everything else is accidental.

Even one big principle, digested and assimilated, can govern and motivate a person for a lifetime. If so many teen-agers today are ungovernable and unmotivated may it not be due to the fact that somewhere along the line we have failed to give them some one big principle of life? Why is there such a tragic paucity of leaders in American social and political life today? Could it be that something *big* was left out of their adolescent training? If so many of our practicing

Catholics are dull, drab, dreary Christians, untouched by the towering greatness of Christ and the holiness of His Father — our Father — is it not in large measure due to an almost exclusive concentration on accidentals — threshold activities — and missing the big essentials — the heart of the matter?

Most people who today possess a religious vocation, an apostolic mission, a burning love of Christ, a sacred, glorious concept of marriage, can trace back the beginnings of it to something in their adolescence — a book, a retreat, a sermon, a person, an event. Something *real*, some *big* ideal, had a devastating impact on them and they have never been quite the same since. What are some of the basic attitudes we must convey to teen-agers?

In general, it may be put this way: there is a threefold, fundamental, irrepressible drive in all young people for LIGHT, LOVE, AND LIFE. And it is in terms of these attractive, dynamic, compelling aspects of human life that they should come to know and feel and grasp Christianity.

LIGHT

They want and need *to see* the mysteries of Christianity as clearly and deeply as possible. They want to know — and should know — the reasons for religious duties and obligations, ethical manners and restraints, social customs and conventions. They want to get to "the bottom of religion," the heart of the Church, and they will not be stayed off, they will not settle for crumbs. They want to see God, they want and need — oh how desperately! — to *know* God *by experience*. And that is the soul of religion, the heart of the Church.

Show that this is *really* what they are looking for, that this is ultimate reality; everything else is a shadow or a sample of this substance. Show how revealed truth is light and food for the mind. "Man does not live by bread alone, but by every word that proceeds from the mouth of God." The

words God utters — commands for our action, truths for our
seeing — are more life-giving, more nourishing, even than the
bread which nourishes the body. For the intellect exists
to know truth and nothing else can nourish it. Supreme
truths God must reveal and then they nourish.

One thing about food — it nourishes only those who eat
it. Only the truths which the mind has digested can nourish
it. The theology which you know does not nourish them
until they, too, learn it. And their soul's *personal* need of
nourishment is as great as yours.

Truth is light. Possessing it, we see reality as it is, we
live mentally in the real world. What eyes *can't* see, we see.
The greater part of reality cannot be seen by the eyes. This
is an important point for teen-agers. Exemplify it: the thing
they see and scream at every morning in the mirror is a
flimsy, fleeting thing — what they see changes every seven
years. There's not a bit of that body left. And yet the same
inner ego remains. And so the enduring, real, precious thing
cannot be seen with bodily eyes.

Moreover, the greater part of reality can be known only if
God reveals it. Those who do not know the things that can
be known only by revelation are living merely in a suburb
of reality; it is pathetic that they should think they are living
in the whole of it.

Thus the person cut off from revealed truth is living an
unnourished life in the dark; is, in fact, half dead. Teen-
agers must do more than accept doctrine. The inner meaning of it must be seen, grasped, lived; otherwise it is
impossible to be nourished by it or gain light from it.

The saints in heaven are full of infinite happiness and
hilarious delight because they see God. We achieve happiness in the world to the extent that we come to see God. But
God is pure spirit and cannot be seen by man. That is why
God became man. Christ is the epiphany of God, the em-
bodiment of God. There is, therefore, hardly anything more

imperative for the retreat master than to make Christ real to his retreatants. Everything depends upon this.

LOVE

Teen-agers want, above all, to be loved. If they can become convinced of God's personal, unchanging, intense love for them, then they can be led gradually and graciously to face calmly and squarely all the demands of conscience, religion, and society. But the fact that God loves them must be the beginning. "And this is charity, not as though you have first loved God but that He has first loved you."

The tremendous reality that God is their Father in heaven will change their lives, once it is accepted. That He cares, that He understands, is the only solution to all the changing moods of youth, their feelings of being misunderstood, their doubts and anxieties for the future. Christ, the self-revelation of the Father, must be made a vivid and ever present reality in their lives. His personal love for them, His physical presence, His loving invitation to "Come to Me all of you and I will refresh you" — this must be a big conviction in their lives.

At this point, simplify all of religion, Christianity, by pinpointing the absolute primacy of love of God. Show how, supernaturally, this is everything, how all other virtues and all other religious acts, all other achievements however great, are valuable only to the extent that they either cause, preserve, or intensify love of God. They have no other reason. Show how all human acts, all of the time, must be charged and permeated with love of God or they are wasted acts. Explain how to make everything an act of love and emphasize the importance of the morning offering, renewed as vitally and actively as possible all day long. Speak strongly, ardently of the world-wide effect of love of God as well as the personal consequences.

Make them think of perfection in terms of love. Make

them see this: Christ commanded *all* to be perfect as God is perfect. All have the same goal, the same obligation, contracted at *baptism* — perfection. A thing is perfect when it fulfills the purpose for which it was created. A gun is perfect when it shoots accurately, a knife is perfect when it cuts cleanly, a man is perfect when united to God. What unites a man to God? Love. So when a man's love of God is perfect he is perfect. It's that simple. To be perfect, love of God must be as deep as possible and as wide as possible. *Deep* means intense, undivided, no reservation, no bargaining, no holding back. *Wide* means *all* of God's creatures (the whole world) are loved in God and for God. No opposition or competition between Creator and creature.

LIFE

Here is where you convey the real Christian message, the stuff of life. Teen-agers want to live life to the hilt. And that is why God became man: "I have come that you may have life, and have it more abundantly." Teen-agers are in relentless pursuit of a gay life, good life, a full life. They are violently opposed to whatever would hinder, hamper, or deprive them of this fullness of life. And so you can imagine — if you have not seen — how they react to religion in the accentuated and exaggerated terms of laws, prohibition, obligations, and morals.

You must make them see Christianity as it is: a thrilling adventure, a love affair between God and man, a life — the most dangerous, mysterious, and joyous life in all the world.

Then turn all of your attention on them, and get them to think of themselves just as they are, restless, lively, unsatisfied, and convince them that as such they are ripe and ready for divine life; that their fury, their fundamental zest for life is the best possible foundation for Christian greatness, holiness, sanctity.

Pick out a few saints and show how and why they were

the boldest and most daring people in the world — Joan of
Arc, Maria Goretti, Francis of Assisi, and others.

Call their attention to the people our Lord takes special
pains to commend — the pagan centurion, the woman who
was a sinner in the city. To whom does He promise paradise?
The thief on the cross. And the heroes of His best-loved
parables are the prodigal son (who, in the words of a third
grader: "left home a dude and came back a bum"), and the
good Samaritan. It is the Scribes and Pharisees with their
pretentious fidelity to the law whom He denounces. "I
would thou wert cold or hot. But because thou art luke-
warm, and neither cold nor hot, I will begin to vomit thee
out of My mouth."

They must see God's plan for them: divine union, infinite beatitude, vision, joy. But they must see, too, that God
does no violence to their nature, that grace builds on nature.
God takes them as they are, and leads them graciously,
gradually to the towering heights of sanctity.

And so a good, solid, healthy, happy nature is a terrific
beginning. But this purely natural life is a puny, piddling
sort of thing that is going to die down and peter out — today,
tomorrow, or forty years from now.

Here speak of death, illness, misery — all the consequences
of original sin. Make them realists. Don't let them escape
(mentally) from the hard facts of life.

Then sweep them up into a brand new realization of the
most glorious, wonderful fact of all: that God has raised
them to supernatural life, has empowered them to live with
divine life and never die. Give them a new fresh idea of
"grace" — the word is so used and worn it has become a
bromide. "Supervitality" might help if used sometimes in
place of "grace."

St. John calls it THE LIFE as if human life by contrast
were not even life. "If thou wouldst have life, go sell what
thou hast and give to the poor and come follow Me" — this

Christ said to the rich young man who had life; he was wealthy, virtuous, young. Obviously, Christ was offering much more. And yet the grace of Christ does not isolate or exclude us. It makes all our human endeavors come magnificently alive. Everything is ennobled, enriched. Everything is transfigured with divine love.

Here you can give them a much more mature outlook and grasp of all the implications of their religion. Otherwise they may remain permanently immature. They must grow up into an "adult Catholicism." Catholicism amounts to infinitely more than they have ever suspected.

The biggest, the most central idea, the one you ought to begin with is "supernatural life" or "sanctifying grace."

Explain this in terms that are obvious and clear. Vegetable life cannot live like animal life, animal life cannot live like human life. Wouldn't it be something if some fine morning the flowers in our gardens would sing like birds and the cat would comment on the weather or the quality of her food? They would be acting above their own natures — SUPERNATURALLY.

We can only imagine this but God can arrange it. He hasn't done it, as far as we know, with plants and animals. But He has done it with man. He has invited him to share divine life which belongs by nature to God alone. That is what GRACE is: we become God by participation; we share His nature, His life, His happiness, His activity, His perfections.

The first consequence is that when we are given grace we cease to be merely ordinary men and women and become, as it were, supermen. We are lifted above the natural plane on which all other creatures exist, and are brought into the closest intimacy with God Himself. For, without ceasing to be God's creatures, we become also God's sons. Having life from God we are really sons of God — not by way of convention, but in fact.

The second consequence is that being sons of God, we are heirs to heaven. If we die in sanctifying grace, to heaven we shall go. If not, we cannot go to heaven simply because we do not have the powers necessary to live there. Natural intellect and will are not enough. We need supernatural life, supernatural powers of knowing and loving.

The "good tidings" of supernatural life is the essence of the Gospel. Grasping this vital notion gives the key to our creed, spirit to our law, and heart to our worship. The doctrine of sanctifying grace illuminates, informs, and enlivens our whole religion. Unless this grips the mind and motivates a man, his religion will be an empty, unimpressive, dead thing — a collection of commands and warnings and restrictions, a bundle of aids for avoiding sin and a pile of merits for self-advancement. And such is a caricature of religion.

Explain with immense clarity and some excitement the key doctrine of the divine indwelling. Point out ways of practicing the presence of God. This is the best way to avoid sin. Awareness of God and of oneself and others as temples of God creates reverence. And if we were always reverent, we would never sin. Sin is violence.

Show them how the possession of supernatural life means being alive to God, being Christ-conscious just as the faithful dog is master-conscious; it means that the thought of God is at the apex of our minds overflowing all the time into our desires, thoughts, actions. It is like a taste in the mouth, a perfume in the nostrils, that conditions, for the time being, the whole of our experience. Being alive to God means that every thought of ours is haunted by the divine presence.

The dullest people in the world, the intolerable bores, the unhappiest people are the selfish individuals who are alive only to themselves, regarding all other people and things in relation to themselves, valuing only those aspects of reality which minister to their pride, their profit, or their pleasure.

Their ego, their dear old ego, like the sun, is too much to look at directly, but throws its light on all the things they do look at. The world for them is bathed in the sunlight of their own point of view.

That is why St. Paul urged the Christians *to be alive to God;* that God instead of self ought to be the center of reference, ought to be the sun that lights up the world for them. And so he adds: "I would have you all aglow with the Spirit . . ." always on the boil. To be aglow with the Spirit means to be a burning and a shining light, to be filled through and through with divine light and fire.

The question that now rises quite naturally and spontaneously to the retreatants' minds is: "where and how do we get supernatural life and how does it grow in us?" In answering these questions you have an opportunity to convey a deeper, clearer notion of the Mystical Body, the Mass, the sacraments, and self-denial. They must come to understand that it is only through the Mystical Body that we acquire our personal share in the divine life; and that it is within the Mystical Body that our personal activities in the supernatural order produce real, live men. There are real, live men outside the Church; but it is the bread of the Church on which they feed and grow.

Begin with physical life of Christ. He is the one single, unique instance in the history of the world of a person born wholly and completely alive. Now, this most remarkable thing — a man so uniquely full of divine life — could never be repeated. There is, then, just one source of infinite eternal, divine life in the world. And that source is accessible to us. If you want to get wet, you get into the water; if you want to get warm you get close to the fire. Well then, if you want to possess the life of God — the gifts, perfection, glory, and splendor of God — then you've got to get into the unique source, into the one, single person who's got all this — Jesus Christ, Son of God.

But how is Christ accessible to us? Did He not die hundreds of years ago? Did He not rise from the dead and ascend into heaven?

Yes. But on the cross His Mystical Body was born. The Church is His Mystical Body. And we are members of the Church; therefore we are His Body. He is the Vine, we are the branches.

So the Church is Christ — the source of supernatural life in the world. Christ lives and acts, glorifies His Father and redeems the world through His Church. And we get into the Church, become His Body, share His divine life by baptism. This divine energy — grace — grows in us and makes us more and more like Christ through all of the other sacraments. And the divinizing process of the sacramental life reaches its unspeakably wonderful climax in the celebration of the Eucharist, the Mass. This great action, so full of life and love and light, has got to be made meaningful and attractive to teen-agers. They love drama — and here is the supreme incident of it in all the world.

Supernatural life is forced upon no one. It is offered. And once received it doesn't evolve automatically. It involves a give and take sort of venture. It works through the principle of loss and gain, through death to life over and over again until there is nothing more to die and all is life.

The meaning and purpose of self-denial can easily be explained here. And ought to be! How simple, for instance, to point out here how the chemicals, moisture, and phosphates of the earth would never know what it means to grow like a plant and enjoy vegetable life unless they first gave up their lower level of lifeless existence. Unless plants are swallowed up in death they will never come to see, hear, and feel, and traverse the earth according to the higher level of animal life. And, unless animals abandon themselves to sacrificial death at human banquets they will have no part in the human life of knowledge and love. And so unless a human being is willing to forsake a purely natural existence for a supernatural existence, he cannot share the life of God, he cannot possess the Kingdom.

Remember what our Lord said: "trade till I come." We actually give up nothing; we exchange something puny for something great, something temporal for something eternal. It is as if Christ stood before us and said: "Give Me your time and I will give you My greatness. Give Me your weakness and I will give you My strength. Give Me your nothingness and I will give you My All."

Within the sacramental context the retreat master ought to make very clear and forceful the fact that the lay apostolate is a normal and necessary part of the Christian life. Make them *feel* their responsibility and direct them toward possible concrete expression of their Christian concern.

The priest should make the concept of "the whole Christ" the central part of his retreat, the chief source of motivation and rule of conduct, bringing up the Two Great Commandments to their proper place, giving our Lord's New Commandment, and showing how positive love of God and neighbor is the way to fulfill the law as a Christian.

Moreover, we must remember how St. Paul derives his Christian morality from the doctrine of the Mystical Body, and in particular from baptism. Be pure, because you are members of Christ. Do not lie or steal, because you are members of another. This positive morality is linked up with our communion with Christ and with one another, and with the sacraments. This is the sort of instruction given to young members of Catholic Action — with amazing results. St. Paul's treatment of morality should surely find its place in a teen-age retreat.

PART II

RETREAT MATERIAL
(In Particular: Teen-Agers)

CHAPTER IV

Horror for Sin

So far, the basic retreat material has been discussed in general. But there are some *particular* topics that are of capital importance and ought never to be omitted from a high school retreat.

Horror for sin, is the first indispensable subject. This is so vastly important because, as Pope Pius XII has said, "The modern world has lost the sense of sin." The commonness of sin is wilting and paralyzing teen-agers' thinking. Even if they *know* what the catechism says about sin, very few seem to admit that it's true. At least they don't *live* it. By every kind of vivid example we must force them to accept, admit, and live all that we teach of the horrible effects of sin.

Make them see how unattractive, how ugly a sinner really is. If every Christian were always mindful of what a sinner looks like to God, none would ever commit a single mortal sin. If every sinner remembered that this is how he once looked, he would never stop doing penance.

You can spell out cogently how and why the sinner is a *coward,* a *hypocrite,* an *ingrate,* a *cruel man,* and a *fool.*

Let them see by various examples how pagan are their attitudes about sin. *Force* them to admit in their own minds how pagan is their thinking. Present them with powerful portrayals of the consequences of sin (1) in loss of peace of mind, (2) in their present and future lives; mention, for instance, the physical consequences of drinking, impurity, stealing, bad companions, bad reading and the like. Get across the idea that a sin has devastating, injurious effects on a person even after the sin has been forgiven in the sacrament of penance. Sin does not merely sully the soul; it twists and contorts it, it is a maladjustment of the whole person. And it takes long, arduous, virtuous labor to righten, straighten, and properly adjust the personality after the staggering effects of sin. (3) Finally, there is the loss of sanctifying grace and the danger of eternal damnation.

An emphasis in the following direction seems helpful: Suppose you have one mortal sin and have no way of its being forgiven, no way of getting sanctifying grace restored to your soul. Suppose there were *no confession!* Suppose you had *just one opportunity* to confess! Suppose you had to go to *one* priest over in Rome! Suppose the penance had to be very severe! Suppose there were *no seal of confession!* "Suppose" a lot of things to let them see how they've grown used to confession and lost the sense of wonder that ought to make it, each time, one of the big, transforming events of their lives.

Pull them away from the tendency toward excessive legalism in their confessions and examination of conscience. They waste time and energy in an exaggerated concern over what is a sin and what kind of a sin, and the like. Drive their thinking deeper — to the essence of sin: a breakdown of love of God, a betrayal and denial of Christ; lead them to the bottom of sins committed and confessed over and over again. What does God think of me *now*, my basic bad dispositions, attitudes, habits?

This whole question on sin and confession will be further developed in the chapter on "The Theme."

CHAPTER V

Personality Development

The meaning and importance of *character* is the other indispensable, particular retreat matter for teen-agers. This should be one of the most important talks in a retreat. There are a number of things that have got to be put across clearly, trenchantly. What is character? A life dominated by principles. What are principles? Strong, basic, sacred rules that govern human behavior despite opposition, public opinion, human respect, despite the world, the flesh, and the devil. Principles are deep-seated, unchanging in convictions, "mindsets" like Maria Goretti's: "death rather than sin," or St. Paul's: "I can do all things in Him who strengthens me." And so insist strongly on the necessity and importance of living by principles. By very vivid, living examples force them to admit the great importance of *character* for salvation. Even God's grace cannot, will not violate our nature. Sanctifying grace can be lost half an hour after confession unless it is firmly built on the natural foundation of a good character.

It is regrettable but true that the strongest force in the lives of too many teen-agers is not the home or church or school; it is, rather, the pull of the *crowd* or the momentary urge or thrill. If we are going to save our young people for the future and prevent them from enslavement to selfish impulses and crowd compulsions, and fortify them against sin and the loss of the friendship of God — then we must make them see the value of character, the imperative need for and attraction of a life dominated and controlled by principles.

It is a good idea, today, to wrap up this whole idea of character in a talk on "Personality Development." Modern teen-agers are thoroughly engaged by anything put in terms of "personality." But it is not only fascinating; it is quite necessary.

They want to be emotionally mature — men and women in the full sense. A deep, didactic treatment of this question is useless and would defeat the purpose. A much better idea is to beat out with successive, repetitive, meaningful words and phrases — like drumbeats — the advantages of maturity and the disadvantages of immaturity, the way to full-grown adulthood and the way to permanent childishness.

Something as bare as the following might be suitable:

FRUITS OF MATURITY

Unselfishness — Thoughtfulness of others, readiness to listen and not monopolize conversation, noting what pleases others, giving rather than receiving attitude, tolerance, courtesy, tact, graduation from egoism, and competitiveness to co-operativeness and the feeling for the human enterprise.

Personal Responsibility — Thoughts for others as a group, concern for the big issues of the world, for the common good, success, reputation of the family, school, society. Willingness to sacrifice some private goods (desires, pleasures, conveniences, comforts, time) for the common good. Obedience, loyalty, fidelity, honesty, respect, healthy independence.

Moderate Emotional Reactions — Emotions are valuable assets to personality. Must be expressed but controlled. Christ showed fear, pity, even though He had absolute control of His emotions. Emotional problems upset our judgments. But emotions, controlled, get things done in the world.

Examples of uncontrolled emotions: wild anger, fear or laughter, undue questioning and hesitation, impulsiveness, impatience, moodiness, prolonged nursing of injured feelings, exploding over small offenses, weeping spells, sulking spells.

One must realize that hostile aggressiveness, anger, hate, cruelty, and belligerency are weakness, and that *kindness, gentleness,* and *good will* are strength.

Profiting by Criticism — Be humble, modest, sincere. Be grateful to critics. Be truthful with oneself. No man is a judge in his own case. Be capable of discussing things calmly, objectively. Seek counsel.

Facing Reality — Distinguish fact from fancy. Stand on own two feet. Use abilities and admit inabilities. Participate with enthusiasm and satisfaction in the gifts and talents of others. Accept frustration and disappointments. Learn by mistakes and failures. Be flexible and adaptable to the changes dictated by fate and fortune. Learn when to be resigned. Always be cheerful and pleasant.

See life as a whole. Faulty adjustment to difficult situations could cause inferiority or an overdependence complex. Reality is the job of the moment — God's will. Finish one job at a time. Do it well. Be willing to undertake anything.

Some questions:
1. Do I try to get out of a job I don't like?
2. Do I crack up in a new situation that will force me out of a rut?
3. Am I given to daydreaming?
4. Do I always find poor excuses for my failures?
5. Do I tend to do first things first?
6. Do I dread responsibility?
7. Do I escape the present by recourse to past or future?

Decisive Thinking —Make decisions and abide by them despite difficulties, pressure, etc. Know yourself and your vocation as soon as possible and then pursue it unremittingly. The need for immediate goals, personal objectives for continuity and achievement. The glory of God, perfection, sanctity are motives that are too general and vague — must be broken down, delimited into concrete, specific, personal, distinct, unique goals that will shape all of one's thinking and behavior.

Balanced Attitude to Sex — Understanding the goodness, beauty, sacredness, the law and limitations of sex. Face sex openly, calmly, reverently. Know the meaning and purpose of sex. Know the normal principles that apply to normal sex life. Accept it as a sphere of life necessary to a well-rounded life. Absence of this calm, objective awareness could cause morbidity, embarrassment, fear, and could hinder a mature growth. Ninety-five per cent of people are exposed to bad sex instruction from ignorant or evil-minded people, stupid, salacious magazines, books, pictures, and movies, and must be re-instructed for chastity.

The Church believes chastity should be taught by proper person, at the proper place and time. Sex information is a parental duty. Sex instruction should gradually increase as the child grows and inquires. Detailed instructions should never be given in a group but separately. No sex instructions should be given without stressing purity and chastity.

Anything a retreat master can do to help young people *understand themselves* will be extremely worthwhile and the retreatants will be forever grateful. He ought, therefore, to point out how they are children of Adam and consequently a bit absurd, rather unreal. He can show them how unreal and unhealthy their human behavior frequently is. One of the most regular patterns of behavior is this: *not getting what you want — suffering some frustration, conflict — seeking some solution.*

In search of a solution the personality resorts to a bag of tricks:

1. Compensation — if I can't have this, I'll take this — can be good or bad.

2. Rationalization — making it look good in the mind — always bad.

3. Idealization — overvaluing something or yourself — conceit.

4. Displacement — taking it out on others.

5. Projection — the other fellow's fault.

6. Conversion — energy of a desire unexpressed is transferred to a physical symptom or complaint — ulcers, for example.

Here are some *signposts for personality trouble:*

1. anxiety
2. depression
3. excitement (constant)
4. withdrawal
5. queer behavior

And for *preventing* troubles the following ought to be considered:

1. relationship with others
2. codes of behavior — principles, intelligence, self-control
3. sources of satisfaction:
   a) new adventure, activities
   b) have you learned the joy of reading?
   c) have you ever created something of your own?
   d) have you a hobby?
   e) friends? plans?
4. obtaining security — feeling comfortable inside yourself
5. the value of your goal — in life, in school, in your job

CHAPTER VI

Human Relationships

Having caught their interest by speaking of personality development, you now show how this is achieved primarily by good human relationships, especially charity and purity. In this context purity is seen in its right perspective: as a positive virtue and as secondary to charity.

So you begin with charity.

FRATERNAL CHARITY

Loving one another is the acid test of whether or not one loves God. There is nothing our Lord spoke so trenchantly about as the need to love one another.

The Eucharist is the sacrament of love, bond of unity, oneness. It is spoiled by division, disunity, unforgiveness. Participation in the Eucharist ought to be characterized by banquet attitudes: conviviality, congeniality, togetherness, joy.

The Final Judgment will be made in terms of love: "What you did to the least of My brethren you did to Me." We already know, then, what our final judgment will be. It's a question of loving one another.

What is commanded by the commandment of love? Never to think, say, or do anything that would hurt another human being.

The command is also positive: To be concerned about other human beings. God indwells them. Christ died for them. All demand reverence, respect.

Sins against charity are the worst kinds of sins. Sins of the spirit are worse than sins of the flesh. One who deliberately engages in gossip can be worse than a prostitute.

The two big problems for most people are: criticism and natural antipathies. Both disorders can be overcome.

Criticism is overcome by the realization of certain facts:
1. All creatures are limited, imperfect. One must be careful about chiding God for the way He made creatures.
2. God alone is limitless and perfect. Refuge must be sought in Him.
3. The human person is the most mysterious and unknown thing in the world. One must be in awe of the human being and not judge rashly, rushing in where angels fear to tread.

A natural antipathy is overcome in two ways:
1. "Where there is no love put love and you will find love."
2. Act *as if*. Act out love and kindness forcefully, deliberately, sincerely, until, by repeated acts, it becomes a habit.

PURITY

The virtue of purity must never be omitted since sins of impurity are the most common sins of teen-agers, or, to put it more accurately, the things they are exposed to make the practice and preservation of purity extremely difficult. The virtue should not, however, be overemphasized, nor the problem exaggerated. Teen-agers resent this. There ought to be at least one conference on purity (sex, dating, and related topics), no more than two.

This conference must be very carefully planned. If not thoroughly and delicately thought out and masterfully expressed, it may do more harm than good. It has to be clear, positive, and balanced.

It would be hard to improve on Fr. Lord's outline:

1. Purity is not a negative virtue.
2. But it is the strong protection which a clear-seeing and strong-willed man and woman
3. Throw around the great creative power of sex, upon the correct use of which depends the whole future.
4. A power entrusted by the Creator to His children
5. As the means of peopling earth and filling heaven.
6. This power, because it demands hard things in the long and tedious bearing of children, is, when properly exercised, rewarded by God, and that reward is mutual attraction, love, and passion.
7. God thought all this sufficiently important and sacred to consecrate it with a sacrament.
8. Hence sin against this power is terrible because:
   a) It betrays the creative power and imperils the whole future.
   b) It steals the rewards of love without accepting the responsibilities for which those rewards were given.

Now discuss clearly, candidly, with ease and delicacy, the *adolescent problem of growing up.* Urge realism and calmness and reverence.

Emphasize the beauty, power, and sacredness of sex.

Explain why some people take a vow of chastity. Be positive.

Spend some time and effort killing the fallacy that is playing such havoc among teen-agers, namely: the effort of entertainers, authors, writers, artists to portray *lust* as delightful and swashbuckling. This is the theme of too many of our pocket books, our comics, our new novels, movies, and TV programs. Movie ads-men love to describe their product as "lusty." And so teen-agers are easily convinced that virtue (especially chastity) is dull. The attitude is summed up by Dorothy Parker: "Whatever I want to do is either illegal, immoral, or fattening."

That fallacy must be destroyed. De-throne lust: it is

sexual-passion-out-of-control. There is nothing glorious about the Columbia river flooding its banks, destroying homes and lives; nothing glorious about the atom or hydrogen bomb going out of control. And neither is there anything admirable about passion out of control: the miser, the liar, the food glutton, the sex glutton are all brutal, savage, vulgar, and inhuman.

Neither is uncontrolled passion, lust, a sign of love. The sensual man, the roué, is not a great lover. He can hardly love at all. He merely seeks his own pleasure by his violent use, abuse, of other people. Real love is a selfless dedication to the other person, involving respect, restraint, reverence, awe. Reverence is always a sign and test of love.

Chastity is not a weakness, but a strength (virtue-manliness). Chastity guards, protects, governs bodily-love-in-action (sex) according to God's law. It exerts this control in two ways: nonuse of sexuality before marriage, and proper, lawful use in marriage.

Chastity, therefore, does not destroy passion, it channels and directs it to its glorious end. It controls vehement, intense passion and makes it serve not lust, but love.

What Is a Sin of Impurity?

Any deliberate sexual pleasure directly consented to outside of marriage is always a serious sin.
1. Alone:
    (a) in thought,
    (b) in action.
2. With others:
    (a) girl,
    (b) boy.

Some Helpful Facts:
1. Thoughts in themselves are not sinful unless deliberately caused or accepted.

2. Most of one's trouble is brought on by oneself — the things one reads, sees, or talks about.
3. Temptations are best overcome by being calm, casual, but firm. A change of place, thought, and occupation if possible.
4. Whatever happens in a dream or while one is asleep cannot be sinful.
5. Today's knowledge does not affect yesterday's sins.
6. One may not act in doubt. One may not do what he thinks might be sinful until he has cleared up the doubt.

Some Questions:

Is it a sin to kiss a girl or to let a boy kiss you?

No, not if it is a gentle, reverent expression of love.

Yes, if it involves passion, deliberately caused and consented to; and if it is at all intense or prolonged it invariably does involve passion. The girl must not think of herself alone. The boy is more passionate by nature. She must consider him.

Any situation, therefore, which by its nature is passionate, is an occasion of sin — such as parking (ordinarily) and petting and necking always.

Is It a Sin to Go Steady?

If this means going exclusively with one person for a long period of time and not in preparation for marriage, then it could easily be an occasion of sin, and frequently is.

It is not only bad morally, but also socially and psychologically.

A CATHOLIC PSYCHIATRIST PROPOSES
14 NEW CUSTOMS FOR DATING

New Rules:

Here are some of the rules he proposed:

1. Going steady is a preparation for marriage and should

not, ordinarily, be permitted to teen-agers. Going steady means going with one partner to the exclusion of others.

2. Going steadily is usually all right if it continues to be just that. "Going steadily" means that a boy and girl agree to go together to the more or less formal affairs, but go with others at other times.

3. When a date is arranged the boy should come to the house to pick up the girl and meet her parents, at least on the first date. He should not sit outside and blow the horn.

4. When the couple leave the house they should have a definite destination and state their expected time of return.

5. If the couple cannot return at the time expected, they should call and report why.

6. No car driving should be permitted until the driver is old enough and actually has a driver's license. "Unfortunately," the Doctor said, "many parents are accessories in this violation of the law."

7. No dating on school nights. When there is no school the next day and they have a date, the couple should return at a "reasonable hour." A "reasonable hour" is one long enough after the end of the function which they attended for a couple to get a "quick bite" at the nearest restaurant and return home.

8. All parties should be chaperoned. Unchaperoned parties "are the product of the confused interpersonal relationships of our times and should not be permitted," he said.

9. Mixed parties for grammar school children are psychologically unsound and should be forbidden by the parents. Formal dancing schools are an exception.

10. Grammar school children as a rule, especially in large cities, should not be out after dark unless accompanied by responsible adults.

11. Solitary dating by grammar school children should be forbidden. Especially undesirable is permitting teen-agers to date older men.

12. No drinking, even of beer, should be permitted at high school parties. This rule, the Doctor said, is frequently violated.

13. Petting (and necking) should be absolutely forbidden.

14. Parents should co-operate in the enforcement of school regulations. For example, although sororities and fraternities are forbidden in most Catholic high schools, parents co-operate in violating this rule by giving their children money for dues. Parents should also insist that their children observe the Legion of Decency list.

Are Mixed Marriages Wrong?

Yes, because of a basic discrepancy which ordinarily is not sufficiently overcome to provide for happiness of family and Catholic education of children.

AVE MARIA STATISTICS
1958
MIXED MARRIAGES

1. Half of 400 mixed marriages give up religion.
2. Divorce and separation 3 times higher.
3. 40 per cent invalid.
4. Both Catholic parents — 92 per cent of the children practicing faith.
   Both Protestant — 68 per cent of the children practicing faith.
   Mixed — 34 per cent of the children practice either faith.
5. Catholic women more likely to enter mixed marriages.
6. Promises are not kept in about 30 per cent of mixed marriages — clue to number of children lost to faith as result.
7. Because of about 85,000 mixed marriages a year 20,000 persons will disappear from active parish life.

CHAPTER VII

Vocation

A vocation talk is absolutely necessary. Young people are terribly mystified by a vocation; and the mystery of it causes uneasiness, alarm, frustration, rash action. And so the subject of vocation demands close, intelligent discussion.

It is never wise to discuss religious vocation alone or even apart from the other states of life or apart from vocation in general. They will get the suspicion you are fishing for them and so become antagonistic or, at least, fearful.

A good approach is to begin the talk from the point of view of the vocation of a *man* as such, or a *woman*, or a human being.

The following is an example:

VOCATION OF WOMEN

It is now time to change the world. Some years ago, Whitaker Chambers, famous ex-communist, wrote a book entitled *The Witness*. In that book he says that the statement — *it is now time to change the world* — is the underlying concept, the great big idea that is the cause and source of all of communism's extraordinary zeal and zest.

And it is true. It is now time to change the world. But communism can never change it; neither can any other "ism" or any other force or power that is merely human, natural, or material. The struggle that we are going through is basically a supernatural struggle between God and Satan;

between Christ in His Mystical Body, the Church, and evil as it has become embodied in the minds and hearts of men. And this kind of problem can only be solved by a power that is supernatural, divine. Now, there is only one institution in the world that wields divine power — and that is Christianity.

Why, then, has Christianity apparently failed? Why has it had such a slight impact on society? Before Christianity can really influence the world it has to come alive in individual people; it has to be made practical and concrete in the everyday lives of real live persons; it has to radiate through them in their home and on their streets, in their schools, factories, offices, courts, and playgrounds.

Our need is for a lived Christianity; for wholehearted, full-fledged Christians. And of these we need, in a special way, women.

No human, no masculine aggressiveness can successfully conclude our crisis; no atomic or hydrogen bomb. These seem only to create fear and tension. They cannot wield divine power. They cannot bear God into the world. They cannot take hold of the healing power of Christ and pour it into the wounds of a dying world.

Such a function has always been the business of womanhood: to be to humanity the bearer of the divine.

When she rears and educates and leads a child to the summit of human perfection, to the pinnacle of all human achievements, divine union, she does something like what made Mary the enviable model of all women, the Mother of all men, and the Queen of heaven and earth. What the world needs is more love less hate, more reverence less aggressiveness. And love and reverence are the genius of motherhood.

Not only mothers are endowed with this power, but all women, which is evident to anyone who has studied the nature of woman and the history of the human race. The

pages of history are bright with examples of women who
exalted and inspired men, but there are also dark pages of
temptation and degradation induced by scoundrels. Kings and
empires have tottered and fallen like crippled things because
of the misused power of women.

This power is one of influence rather than enterprise. Her
power of influence is a frightful responsibility. Like all other
particularly precious gifts of God — physical beauty, wealth,
fire, atomic energy — it must be used for the glory of God
and the good of mankind. If not, it drags man down to hell.
A woman must remember that she cannot live in the world
without influencing it for good or evil. She can raise man
to the stars or drive him into the mire of the earth. Perhaps
she may come into contact with very few people; never-
theless, as St. Francis de Sales used to say: "One soul is a
large enough diocese."

And so a woman has the unique opportunity of redeeming
the world by being herself, her best self; she can if she is
true to the deepest nature, come forward with immense
power to heal humanity and in so doing achieve for herself
immense glory.

That is why they say you must never underestimate the
power of a woman; and the hand that rocks the cradle rules
the world. That is why, so very often, you can trace both
delinquency and greatness back to a woman.

Napoleon was conversant with the power of woman.
When asked what he needed most to save France, his answer made no plea for armies, statesmen, or politicians. He
said simply: "Give me a handful of good holy women and
I will save France." And Pius XI made an almost identical
plea for the Church.

CONTEMPLATION

A woman's influence grows out of her *womanly wisdom.*
Her distinct gift from God is her intuition. It is mysteriously

effective. She does not always have to plod her way into the possession of truth by a slow, logical, and laborious process. She does not even seem to pursue truth by way of the cold, abstract intellect. She seems instead to woo truth into her possession by an ardent, sympathetic reach and stretch of her whole sensitive receptive being. Her intuition of reality is immediate and direct, more a result of love than of reason; but really an intense, heightened actuation of both.

Woman is by nature contemplative rather than activist. Man rules on the surface level. He pontificates in the tempest and on the crest of the waves. Woman, on the contrary, dwells and belongs in the depths. Out of the depths she is out of order, out of her environment, out of touch with the necessary conditions of womanly wisdom, beauty, power.

There is nothing in this world more odious and appalling than a shallow, superficial woman. There is nothing that destroys her beauty, elegance, and power so fast and furiously as a dirty mind or an empty mind, a foul mouth, coarse language, stupid jokes, excessive drinking, cheap actions, hyperactivity, and immodesty.

If a woman is to achieve her full-grown noble stature, then her life must be full of stillness, silence, and serenity. These are the earmarks of a contemplative.

What does it mean to be a contemplative? It means to know God by experience — a pure intuition of God born of love. And women are eminently disposed by nature and disposition for this gift of God. And men expect as much from women. How reverently men would look up to them, how avidly they would listen to them if they would speak out of the profound depths of reality — if they would speak as women who have seen and touched the resurrected Christ!

Women should be educated in this direction: toward the cultivation of their intuitive life, their womanly wisdom. "Mary kept all these words, pondering them in her heart." This is wisdom — to have a right taste for divine things, to ponder them and in the light of these divine things, to judge human things, in a word, perfectly to order.

So you see peace in the home is a fruit of wisdom. Mary, the Mother of Sorrows, was superbly serene despite human tragedies because she judged the human in the light of the divine. She saw the whole of reality against the background of eternity. She beheld the manifold in the One. In other words her contemplative life gave a calm, quiet strength to her active life.

That is why a woman must heed Christ's command: to pray without ceasing. In a family of seven where does a woman find time for prayer? This is the difficulty naturally brought up by a pagan world which does not understand that this thoughtfulness of wisdom, this habit of prayer, is not so much a matter of a quiet day as of a quiet heart; not so much a matter of closed eyes as of eyes wide open; of using the daily demands and relentless routine of family life for plunges into the heart of divine things.

The enemies of the home are the enemies of wisdom — all these things that pull the mind and heart of woman away from divine intimacy, that prevent her pondering divine truths and judging in terms of them. If she loses her *taste for the right things* (wisdom), she loses her womanly beauty and power and forfeits her vocation.

ACTION

A woman must also act; but her action must be simple. Her business is to take care of God and to take care of man. She does this all at once by taking care of Christ in both God and man. Mary is the supreme model of this kind of life. She was completely absorbed in the care of her Son, totally dedicated to His purpose in the world. And so she was perfectly selfless.

In a sense Mary never quite finished her work of love; she has bequeathed to every one of her daughters her own task of love, the joyous task of caring for her Son.

To say that Mary's Son has need of that womanly care is not mere poetic fancy or rhetorical exaggeration. For all the unspeakable clarity with which Paul had seen the completeness of Christ's triumph and the glorious perfection of His nature, he could still speak of the faithful completing the sufferings of the Lord. No such divinely inspired insight is needed to see the necessity for the continual nourishment of the mystical body of Mary's son; yet is that not continuing the work of Mary?

Mary's care of her child is at the same time a statement of woman's apostolate and its demarcation. God did not pull Mary out of a hat. The whole period of the Old Testament was a long, arduous, careful preparation for Mary. She was the epitome of all that took place in the lives of all the great women of the old world. She was the perfect flower that sacred history was meant to produce. No woman just happens to be beautiful, dignified, powerful. It is the result of training; good reading, prayer, mortification, the practice of the virtues. And so her apostolate, like Mary's must be preceded by intense preparation involving personal perfection.

A woman's apostolate will be more intensive than extensive. It will consist, essentially, in bringing God into the world, and the world to God. She, like Mary, must step aside to let Christ do His work. Her work, always an intensely personal affair, as was Mary's, will be quiet, unobtrusive, indispensable.

A woman's apostolate of mercy and pity, care and solicitude always involves pain and suffering. It took seven swords of sorrow to break Mary's heart wide open — to the dimension of the universe, to the compass of Christ's own heart: so that she could embrace the universe and mother all men.

It is impossible to appreciate Christ and not be an apostle. Mary is proof of this. So is Anna the prophetess, the woman at the well, Therese of Lisieux, and Joan of Arc.

What is the most usual expression of a woman's mysteriously effective activity of love? It is *kindness*, stubborn, undying kindness. "Be kind, be kind, be kind, and you will be a saint." This means far more than sweet kindliness, benevolence, superficial well-wishing, back-patting, and the philanthropy that operates on glib publicity and pomposity. It really means willing or desiring the good of another efficaciously.

It is not by throwing her weight around that a woman will accomplish most; but by self-effacement. Her role when offered suffering, silence, success, or glory is to utter her *fiat*: "let it be done unto me." Her vocation is to wait, to suggest, to inspire, and to contemplate; not to command and take the initiative, but to inspire man to command and take the initiative; not to save man but to offer him the courage and wisdom to save himself.

A fine example of how this role is fulfilled is the case of Nathaniel Hawthorne. He came home to his wife one day with the bad news that he had lost his government job. His wife refused to complain or bemoan their fate. Instead she was a column of strength. She was an inspiration and a calm moral support. She was above all kind. She came to his rescue with the creative intuitive force of a woman. She sat Nathaniel down by the hearth, fetched his paper and ink, and said: "Thank God you lost your job; now you have time to write a book." And so he wrote a book — one of the three greatest books ever written in America — *The Scarlet Letter*.

This splendid thing was achieved because a woman played her role so magnificently and managed to be calm, kind, and wise.

In order to be fully effective as a woman, you will need to know as soon as possible — ideally by the end of high school — your particular vocation.

There are three specific states of life: single state, marriage, religious life. Each one is good. No matter which vocation is yours sanctity is still required of you. In fact, there is a more pressing need to be holy on the threshold of marriage than upon entrance to the religious life. One reason is that when you enter religion everyone and everything works to make you holy; but in marriage it is far more up to you. Another reason is that in marriage you are also responsible, to a large degree, for your husband's holiness and for the holiness of your children, and on and on.

How do you know your vocation? Well, frequently it begins with a natural attraction to one particular state of life more than to either of the others. But not always. In fact sometimes there may be an actual repulsion to the whole idea. It need not matter.

Basically, you ascertain your vocation by a *reasonable process*; and this may be in spite of how you feel about it. You ask yourself three questions:

1. In which state will I most surely, readily, quickly, give glory to God?

2. In which state will I most surely, readily, quickly become a saint?

3. In which state will I be most likely to contribute something of value to the world?

The answer to each of these questions will depend upon you and your unique, distinct individuality, upon your talents, background, health, aspirations, interests, and the like.

You may never erase all doubts. No one *really* knows, for instance, that she has a religious vocation until profession day — years after entrance.

But there is a principle you can use to reduce doubt, namely: the more direct and immediate service of God (religious life) gets the preference. It is the state of perfection. In other words, if you have three reasons for not entering religious life and three for entering, and have at the same time health, intelligence, and the will to enter, you should enter. In fact, St. Alphonsus Liguori says that if you have a reasonable, enduring suspicion that you have a religious vocation, then you should enter.

Anyway, during your high school years you should read about each of the vocations; discuss each with adults who are adequately informed and experienced; and pray for light to know your vocation and the courage to embrace it without delay.

CHAPTER VIII

Personal Devotion to Christ

To date, the biggest hole in our educational system is the failure to convey to young students a meaningful, vital awareness of Christ. This conclusion is the result of years of experience. During that time, Catholic high school and college students in all parts of the country were examined as to their impressions and knowledge of Christ, and as to the part He played in their lives. The general response was not good.

Their ideas were vague, general, unreal, sentimental, impersonal, academic. To many Christ was a myth; to others merely a historical figure; to others divine all right, but quite remote and not a fact of everyday life. But a religion without Christ is a corpse; an education that does not convey ideas of Christ that are vital, real, precise, and compelling is a farce. If teen-agers are ready to worship a hero and follow a leader, then it is a mistake to obscure the person of Christ behind a welter of abstractions. If they are going to be raised to a higher stature it will take more than moral coercion or intellectual persuasion, even the high ideal of becoming perfect, a saint.

Such an ideal is too abstract; and a young person needs something concrete, dynamic, highly personal to shape his thinking and influence his behavior. He needs the infinitely attractive personality of Christ. Nothing else will do; for nothing else will catch and hold his attention, engage his interest, and fill his heart as Christ will. Christ lived a life so captivatingly lovable that it is enough to tear the heart out of anyone who will become acquainted with it. Teen-agers cannot help but be influenced by the irresistible force of Him who said: "And I, if I be lifted up, I will draw all things to Myself."

It is impossible to look into the face of Christ without being drawn into the action of Christ. That is what François Mauriac meant when he said: "Once you get to know Christ, you cannot be cured of Him." That is also why you will never see a crucifix in a Discalced Carmelite cell. Every Carmelite wears one on his heart for there is none on the bare walls of the cell; just the empty cross. The reason for this is the difference between the crucifix and the cross. The crucifix is a memorial to a crucified God, but a cross is an invitation to a real Christian. It is the divine call and challenge to do what He did for the glory of His Father and the redemption of the world.

Teen-agers must be taught, therefore, to believe not only in a creed but through a creed in a Person. Faith must come to mean to them what it meant to St. Bonaventure: "a habit of the mind whereby we are drawn and captivated into the following of Christ." Religion will thus become more than a moral code, a list of forbidding commandments, a dull drab affair. It will take on the thrill and excitement of a love affair between God and man. It will mean, above all, a friendship with Christ.

There are two things, therefore, that Catholic education should teach permanently: How and where to read the life of Christ, and how to pray. Only in view of this kind of teaching can there be reasonable hope for teen-agers and adults coming to know God by experience. The following is an example of a *Christ talk* in a high school or college retreat.

Example

What does He mean to you? Have you not been as long as you can remember groping for something that has eluded you, grasping at one thing and then another, captivated again and again by new vistas of life that opened up suddenly, unexpectedly, yet left you at the end, still wandering, disillusioned, restless.

Like all the rest of us you wanted a companion. You could not bear to live alone; you wanted and needed someone with whom to share the adventure of life — the unpredictable joy of it, the inevitable pain of it. And so you attached yourself to another heart the same size as your own, but inevitable conditions of life deprived you of it. Then you went in search for another to lean on, love, and share joy and sorrow with. But there was something fleeting, futile, and unsatisfying about them all.

The secret of it all dawned on you one day. You had been looking the wrong way, searching far off when the soul-satisfying object of your hunger and your striving was within your grasp all the time. All the time you had a companion; "a baby in your babyhood, a child in your childhood, a youth beside your youth — happy when you were happy, sorrowing when you were sorrowful, as triumphant as yourself over your victory; no more than you and yet enclosing you, accepting all the love that you were capable of giving and giving so much more in return; hungering more than you hungered, and putting your hunger to shame; so that henceforth your tiny little hunger forgot its own hunger in its longing to satisfy this other hungry heart whose cravings mattered so much more."

God loves you. He became man to reveal this to you. He died to prove it to you. "Greater love than this no man has than to lay down his life for a friend." And for your sake He did not come down from the cross. His enemies teased

Him to come down. It would have been a terrific moment full of glory and triumph. He could have proved so many things; He could have forced His enemies to eat their words; He could have consoled His Mother, reclaimed His scattered following, and vindicated Himself.

But He did not come down. Why not? He loved you and me. He wanted to walk not only over the hills of Palestine and on the waters of Genesareth; He wanted to walk on hills of New England and the waters of America. He wanted to possess the hearts not only of Mary and Peter and John but all the hearts of all the people in the world for all times.

For this He had to die and come alive again in His Mystical Body with a life just as real and dynamic and influential as was His physical life. "I have loved you unto the end. . . . I am with you all days, even to the consummation of the world." Such is the exigency of love. It is the nature of friends to spend their days delighting in one another. So spoke Aristotle, the philosopher. So lives Christ, the relentless lover.

Have you ever really known what it means to love? Do you know what is love unsatisfied, endured in loneliness, ready to burst your restless, ravenous heart? Do you know what it is to have the intolerable strain suddenly removed, the void suddenly filled up, to have found Him whom your soul has always loved, to have held Him, and never to let Him go?

If not, you have not come to know Jesus Christ. He is the Pied Piper of human hearts. He makes people become like little children, and suddenly turns the world they live in upside down because they have become fascinated and enchanted by Him. He turns human lives inside out like gloves. He transforms weak, hesitant fishermen into strong, ardent champions of God. He makes them walk on water and live as carefree as birds.

Christ is the invisible Piper piping through all the streets

of the world. He is the Catholic Church in the world. Other
religious, social, and political organizations may arouse opposition, but the incurable disquietude of those who fear
the Catholic Church is due to the fact that while all others
are systems, the Church is a Person (collective), an incalculable Person, the Person of Jesus Christ living in His
members.

There is no decent response to His attraction other than
irrevocable commitment. Once you follow Him you no
longer desire to satisfy your own loves, but you desire instead to satisfy with all your life the love of Another. You
no longer seek pleasure in love, but you forget your own
existence in a new ardent love. Your own delight in love is
to suffer and to live in order to give, to endure, to labor.

One day when F. D. Roosevelt was President he is said
to have met a lad on the corner selling newspapers. He
casually asked the little fellow what he planned to do with
the money he made on the papers. The boy answered that
he intended to build a city as large as New York. The
President laughed. The boy went on to explain that it
wasn't so funny or impossible after all because "my buddy
is down on the next corner; and he is also selling papers;
we are working on this thing together."

That was the foundation of his bold and daring project:
working together with a friend. It wasn't quite valid in his
case because his friend was as human as he, and could only
contribute an extremely limited amount to the cause. But
in your case, working together with your friend, Christ, Son
of the living God, is a valid foundation for the most daring,
superhuman endeavors. Like St. Paul, Joan of Arc, Teresa,
and the other saints, you can do all things in Him who
strengthens you, who buoys you up, who has already overcome the world.

It is a unique and unspeakably wonderful kind of friendship. Christ is like you and yet is infinitely perfect. He is so

down to earth and yet God of heaven and earth. He takes delight in your company and yet all creation cannot contain Him. He knows you through and through — your shame, your sinfulness, your cowardice — and yet loves you with an everlasting love. He will never forsake you no matter how repulsive you may become to human company. He will never let you suffer alone, no matter how degraded and despicable your suffering may be. And He will never have a PRIVATE sort of joy or sorrow because of you.

His love has transformed yours, not crushed it. Although you love no one besides Christ, you do love all in Christ. He has not taught you to love things less and less for the sake of His friendship; you have learned to love them more and more as you see them with His eyes and love them with His heart. Now you know what love means; not the cramped, limping, narrowed, self-indulgent thing that so many fancy it to be, but the great, stouthearted, selfless, all embracing thing that opens a man's heart to the dimensions of the universe, shaping it to the compass of Christ's own heart, giving man a certain kinship with God Himself.

CHRIST IS THE IDEAL MAN. You will always be dissatisfied with even the loftiest specimens of mankind. No one of our noblest men is a spotless sun; no one reached sinless perfection, no one except Christ. In Him the ideal becomes actual, the dream real.

He is the fullest manifestation of divinity God had given to the world; He is the brightness of God's glory, and the very image of God's substance. He rises in unapproachable glory, not only above men, but also above saints and seraphs, above angels and archangels. Gazing upon Him we can exclaim with inexpressible enthusiasm and unutterable ecstasy, "He is Man!" and with the same breath and with equal truth we can also reverently exclaim, "He is God!"

Here was a Man who was really what all men were intended to be; and, of course, much more besides. In this single instance, humanity had, so to speak, arrived; had passed into the life of Christ. All of mankind is affected. It makes a difference to people who lived before Christ as well as to people who lived after Him. It makes a difference to people who have never heard of Him. It is like dropping one tiny particle of saccharin into a cup of coffee, giving a new taste to the whole cup.

Do not think of Christ as a dreamy, sentimental, and poetic character. Read a good life of our Lord. Read, for instance, Mauriac or Papini or Ricciotti. Avoid nursery endearments. Christ is the great exemplar, the perfect model, the sublime original to be imitated by all true men and women. In Him and in Him only, the plant of humanity blossomed and blossomed into a perfect flower.

CHRIST HAS A HUMAN NATURE. If we were to write down all the significant data about Christ, "the world," as St. John tells us, "would not contain the books that must be written."

It is easy to see that Christ possessed extraordinary physical charm: children loved Him, and those in any sort of trouble ran to Him. He was strong and virile: He rose very early in the morning to pray and often spent whole nights in prayer; and very often He had nowhere to sleep but the open air. During his public life He always journeyed on foot, and with the minimum of provisions. Sometimes He stayed so long with the sick He took no time to eat.

He had an extraordinary knack of handling crowds. He had to be always on the alert, for His enemies were forever trying to trick Him. Recall this incident: the scene is graphic, the lesson cogent. The Scribes and Pharisees are, as usual, plying Him with questions. Suddenly the tables are turned. Christ halts them, impales their quizzical, lusterless eyes on the fine point of His piercing, irresistible gaze; and He asks them questions.

This was an unforgettable instance among the Jews. Here

was a carpenter's son, an uneducated man from Nazareth, questioning the Doctors of the law, the elite, the intelligentsia. You could have hung your hat on the tension that shot like a tangent from the regal commanding figure of Christ to the encircling gloom of dumfounded men.

The devastating irony with which the evangelist closes his account of the incident is precious: "and from that day on no man ever dared ask Him any more questions."

The closest disciples are often a trial to Christ's patience because of their inability to understand and their narrowness of outlook. He had an insatiable thirst for life. It was to share this zest for life that He came into the world: "I come that you may have life and have it more abundantly."

He lived life to the hilt. Only the strongest and healthiest physique could have borne the strain of so full a life. His last journey from Jericho to Jerusalem through rocky country and a blazing sun, involved a climb of about 3500 feet in six hours; and it was at the end of this rugged haul — that would have exhausted the Fighting Irish at Notre Dame — that He took part in the banquet at Bethany with Lazarus and his sisters.

The exquisite sovereignty of His mind was obvious in every situation at every moment. With clarity and assurance He knew exactly what His mission was. You notice the number of times He says: I come for this or that purpose, I do not come for this other. Never any hesitation, doubt, or compromise. He was always direct, candid, genuine.

Some people are disturbed by the fact that Christ was, on rare occasions, stern and angry; they feel something incompatible between this harshness and the more characteristic gentleness of the Lord. But these qualities are part of the same fullness of the Son of God. If you love humanity, you must hate inhumanity; if you enjoy a perfect vision of truth, you will be that much more thoroughly set against deceit and falsehood. Christ was not just a romantic, sentimental humanitarian, in whom moral indignation and righteous anger would be out of place.

Christ was not an impossible sort of idealist. He loved us unto the end all right; but all the time He was aware of our selfishness, cowardice, and infidelity, the horrible fact of malice, hatred, and gross evil that is in the world. But He was full of pity and mercy, and undying love just the same. Remember the publican, the adulteress, the Lord's gentleness with Judas, and His forgiveness of Peter.

Our Lord's delicate and precise concern for the little things of life is most precious. The roads and fields of Palestine were companions to His life and work. The poor were His delight, and sinners the object of His love and attention. Children seemed to be specially favored creatures of His kingdom. He loves to toy reverently and significantly with trees, flowers, water, wind, sand, and stars. Nothing escapes His love and care.

Jesus is far more than a mere man, far more than even the greatest historical figure. He is God. You can admire and extol historical figures; but you don't fall in love with them. It is impossible to know Christ without falling in love with Him. It is important, therefore to cultivate a sharp awareness of the divinity of Christ. "He that sees Me sees God. . . . Behold a greater than Solomon is here. . . . I tell you there is here a greater than the temple. . . . The Son of Man is Lord of the Sabbath. . . . He that loveth Father and Mother more than Me is not worthy of Me. . . . I am the Bread of Life. . . . I am the Way, the Truth, and the Life. . . . Before Abraham was made, I am. . . . I am the Son of the Blessed One, and you shall see the Son of Man coming in clouds of glory. . . ."

Christ introduced a whole new era into the world — an era of love. He cured the deaf, the blind, the crippled; and He raised the dead to life — all on His own authority. Never in His life did He betray any hint of a personal sense of sin. His prayer, too, is unique: there is complete absence of awe, fear, and penitence; but just the highest pitch of intimate, loving communion — unbroken by spiritual crises and upheavals that you find in other great men of prayer.

No law of heredity can account for the physical attractiveness, the mental superiority, and the moral perfection of Jesus. Neither can environment, nor education. Yet even His enemies were constrained to say: "No man ever spoke like this man." Who else could utter anything akin to the Sermon on the Mount? The foremost thinkers of today barely understand the social and religious significance of the Beatitudes. In pure spirituality of thought it is surpassed only by our Lord's last discourse to His disciples. This farewell address bears the ineffaceable marks of His divinity.

Remember that terrific scene when the Lord is riding triumphantly into Jerusalem and the people are spreading palms before Him and shouting alleluias of praise? Well, as you recall, the big men, the Scribes and Pharisees — envious of this adulation — protested and commanded Christ to forbid such demonstration of loyalty and affection. And it was then that Christ said: "If they should be silenced, the very stones would cry out."

No wonder He had such amazing instantaneous effect upon the disciples. He said to them "Come after Me . . ." and immediately leaving their nets they followed Him. It is as complete and absolute a commitment as that. He is like a potter with His clay.

Do you realize what a tremendous thing it was that He should emancipate Himself from the sectarianism and the sectionalism of His country and century, and become the contemporary of all ages?

Now, this Christ is the God who dwells within you; who is closer to you than you are to yourself; who is more real than you are. You are real to the extent that you are in touch with His reality; you are alive to the degree that you respond to His activity.

What is His activity? Making friends out of human stuff. He is always at it — loving, hounding, wooing, enticing — until there is an adequate response from the human person, which means complete capitulation before the devastating demands of a jealous Lover, absolute surrender to the relentless chase of the Divine Friend.

How does your response shape up? The first element is *knowledge* — a progressive enlightenment of the mind through spiritual reading (especially the life of Christ, more especially the New Testament), intelligent discussion, mental prayer (daily), and the consistent effort to live in the presence of God.

The second is *love*, a gradual enlargement of the heart through desiring, above all things and through all things, the friendship of Christ, through acts of love all day long (accepting everything from God, offering all to God, and sacrificing some things for God), through prayer (liturgical and private), and love of neighbor (not merely by avoiding evil but by a positive, tender care and solicitude).

The third element is *commitment* to Christ: Is your idea of Christ the biggest thing in your mind, or is it smothered and nullified by other ideas you get from movies, magazines, TV, cheap books, and idle chatter? Does He fill your soul like a riot of joy and sit on the edge of your lips like a shout of praise?

From now on you must have one, single reason for everything you do, and that reason must be Christ.

CHAPTER IX

Prayer

No one can come to know and love Christ except by prayer. Prayer more than any other human activity throws faith into action and thus develops that "habit of the mind whereby we are drawn and captivated into the following of Christ." Praying makes all the difference in the world. It's the difference between hearing all about Christ and meeting Him face to face. Prayer is experiential knowledge of God. It is Christian doctrine lived.

In mental prayer faith becomes functional. Information about God becomes conviction. A drab, naked outline of Catholic faith becomes a burning experience. What before was objective truth now becomes also a subjective awareness of truth.

God is someone to speak to, to listen to. Learning to pray is falling in love. In mental prayer truth becomes excitingly interesting. Christ becomes progressively fascinating. God reveals Himself.

So it is vastly important to teach the art of prayer. Yes, it is an art, sad to say. At one time it was the most spontaneous thing in the world. But our first parents lost this easy entree to God when they committed original sin. We are now able to regain this spontaneous communion with God by learning the art of prayer.

The following outline, if filled in appropriately, can be used for any age group.

MENTAL PRAYER

I. *Nature of Prayer*

1. Purpose

To activate and exercise the theological virtues of faith, hope, and love so that by their growth and development we can achieve the goal of human life: union with God.

It is one thing to make isolated acts of faith and love; quite another to acquire the habit of faith and love. This is the function of prayer.

2. Necessity

St. Alphonsus: morally impossible for him who neglects meditation to live without sin.

St. Teresa: He who neglects mental prayer needs not a devil to carry him to hell, but he brings himself there with his own hands. So not a superfluous nicety, but a basic necessity.

Pius XII: It must be stated without reservation that no other means has the unique efficacy of meditation, and that as a consequence, its daily practice can in no wise be substituted for.

Christ came to re-establish God's friendship; and prayer is our principal contact with Him.

That is why St. Paul told the Thessalonians to pray without ceasing.

Prayer is as important for the life of the soul as breathing is for the life of the body.

3. Definition of Prayer

In general — raising of the mind and heart to God.

In particular — a heart-to-heart conversation with God, who we know loves us. Prayer is not having great ideas about God, thrilling feelings, sweet consolations. It is the awareness of God, His reality, His closeness, His love.

4. Method of Prayer { a series of steps used to facilitate the acts of friendship and assist the formation of the habit of prayer.

St. Teresa's method — broad enough for freedom; precise enough for the logical nature of the human mind.

Purpose of method. Like a scaffolding: as house begins to rise (familiarity with God) the scaffolding (formal method) is done away with gradually, until finally, the finished house (friendship with God) has no need of it at all.

Method is a sometime thing.

II. *Explanation of the Method*

1. Preparation — remote and immediate.

2. Imagination — Why do you talk in sleep? But God is pure spirit; we are not; cannot come into His presence the way the angels do. We go by way of senses and imagination. The difficulty of forming an image of God is removed by Incarnation (cf. 1 Jn. 1:1–2).

3. Consideration or meditation — Who is here in this scene? What is He doing? Why? What does it mean to me?

4. The conversation — love, desire, acts of adoration, thanksgiving, reparation, petition, sorrow, determination, complaint, wonder, etc. Silence. Gazing. Waiting. Listening.

5. Conclusion — thanksgiving, oblation, petition.

III. *The Process of Prayer*

Prayer is a spiritual education carried on with the soul as pupil and the Holy Spirit as instructor.

Learning to pray is like learning to read. Tyro readers need lots of pictures to attract them and urge them on. Beginners in prayer need lots of images, etc. But a reader can't go on like that. Neither can a prayer. There must be progress.

But there is a crucial period one has to get through — the period of transition, when God is introducing the soul into the purer regions of prayer, into the first stages of Contemplation.

IV. *Effects of Prayer*

1. Knowledge of God

To pray is to know God by experience.

Christ's momentous question: "What think ye of Christ?" can only be answered by those who pray, who know God experimentally, intimately.

2. Practice of Virtue

Compare catechism or book resolution with face-to-face resolution.

Compare attitude of awe and reverence at Lincoln Memorial or Grand Canyon with petty, callous, and coarse attitude over the back fence.

3. Peace of Soul

Only prayer can make the depths of our souls calm when the surface is stormy and turbulent. Prayer gives us independence of moods in two ways: (1) It exhausts our bad moods by telling them to God. (2) The second advantage of prayer is not only to void our bad moods, but to replace them with good feelings. There is gradual assimilation to Christ through feeling and action — Cum innocente, innocens eris, cum perverso, perversus eris (Ps.).

PART III

A THEME

CHAPTER X

Outline of Theme

It is a good idea to have a retreat theme, a single thread running through all the conferences, giving continuity and unity to the whole thing.

The following is an outline of one possible theme which can be adjusted for the needs, interests, and purposes of any group of retreatants.

I

Theme: God loves you. Your life is a response to God. Your life will be as real, happy, successful, whole — and therefore holy — as you manage to respond first and foremost, above and through all other things, to this basic fact: God's personal love for you.

God loves you. Becoming convinced of that, making it the most influential thing in your life, growing in the consciousness of His love: this is the stuff of sanctity; the driving motivation in the lives of all the saints. Striking example is St. Therese.

Creation as a visible manifestation of God's love

Your existence. You are because God loves you. God's loving care and infinite solicitude. Your complete dependence.

The Incarnation as full manifestation of God's love. God in His most attractive form. Christ's passion and death: "Greater love than this no man has than to lay down his life for a friend."

And so *religion* is a love affair between God and man.

II

Your Response. You come alive as you respond to the high *proposal* of God's love. Suppose a most remarkable and lovable person suddenly came sweeping into your life with extraordinary love, offering you a kingdom — you'd respond. How? First by striving to get to *know* as much as possible about this person who loves you and then by seeking the company of this good friend and benefactor as often as possible. These happen to be the two salient features of a human response; to God: the *search for knowledge* and for *communion.*

Having begun at the beginning — "and this is charity not as though we have loved God, but that God has *first* loved us" — and emphasized God's initiative, His overture, love, pursuit only now can the real *purpose of life* be understood.

The purpose of *all* life is to give honor and glory to God. How? By being what they were meant to be: Trees give glory to God by being trees, fish by being fishy, humans by being as human as possible. When a human being becomes perfectly human he is a saint. But he cannot become perfectly human unless he becomes, in a sense, partly divine (that is, share divine nature). To this end he was supernaturalized, graced, incorporated into the mystical body of Christ. That is why it is nonsensical and inhuman not to be a saint.

What distinguishes the human from every other animal? Knowledge and love. Progressive knowledge and love make up the humanizing process; on the supernatural level it is also the sanctifying process. Perfection, sanctity, salvation are all by-products of giving honor and glory to God by being human; that is, getting to know God so well that one necessarily falls in love with Him. It is this love, knowledge that induces virtue, Christlikeness, sanctity.

III

Sin — Confession. Sin is the only thing that destroys man's response to God. That is why sin is really the *only* evil. All other evil is an effect of this basic rupture in the God-Man relationship.

Impossible to comprehend the horror of sin. But you catch a glimpse of it in the Crucifixion, in the life and death of Judas, in the denial of Peter.

Sin is always a betrayal, a denial, a preference of some creature over against the Creator.

But sin should not depress a person. There is the refreshing, healing sacrament of penance.

There is more than getting rid of sin to confession. There should be gradual spiritual growth through spiritual direction and the positive grace of the sacrament.

Suggestions for getting more out of confession:

1. Do not worry so much about the completeness of your confession, that is, getting in all your venial sins.

2. Do not make a moral case, a court session out of it. It is a personal meeting of love between God and a child of God.

3. Do not worry about or even re-examine past sins. God isn't interested. And it can't come out right anyway. But do not hide a deliberate, willful, mortal sin either.

4. Do not confess *all* your venial sins. You don't have to; and by doing so you spread your sorrow too thin and your reform too wide. Result: no improvement.

5. Ask the priest to suggest a program of reform.

6. Do not promise our Lord you will be better next month or week; just plan your next day. In the morning renew that one resolution, pray for the grace; repeat three times in morning and three times in afternoon; examine your conscience that night; begin all over again the next day.

If you are this concrete and specific about confession, knowing what you want and going in there and getting it, you will be actively and intelligently participating in the sacrament of penance. The result will be spiritual growth.

IV

Mary, the perfect model of the human response to God's love.

What God asked of her: her body and soul, her days and nights, her laughter and labor, her joys and sorrows — the total but simple gift of herself.

How the whole world hung on her response —.

How she responded: "Behold the handmaid of the Lord; be it done unto me according to thy word." *Fiat!* A perfect response.

The effect: she bore God into our world.

Mary saves us from complicating our lives. Her holiness was not achieved by a flight from the world or a withdrawal from society; not by a multiplication of prayers and devotions; not by clever, austere techniques and methods. All Mary did was take good care of Christ.

And that's all you have to do too: take good care of Christ; know Him, love Him; be devoted and committed.

V

The Christ-life. But how can fallen man respond adequately to God the Father's love? By getting into Christ. The Father's only begotten Son is the only one in the whole world who can really respond. If you want to respond to God, you've got to get into Christ and so come to think like Him, love like Him, and act like Him.

That's why Christ instituted His Church, His Mystical Body, the prolongation of the Incarnation, the life of Christ in the world today: so that by baptism you can get into Christ, live His life, pray His prayer, utter His response.

That is what the liturgy is: the prayer of the whole Christ, the response of the Head and all its members.

And so you learn to respond by living the liturgical life, the liturgical year, the Mass in the spirit of Christ, the spirit of sacrifice.

VI

Faith. At baptism you became equipped with brand new superhuman powers for the purpose of responding. These new powers are faith, hope, and charity. Although charity is the greatest of the virtues, faith is the basic and fundamental virtue because you cannot love what you do not know. And, this side of heaven, faith is the only way that you can know God as He is in Himself.

By faith you share Christ's own knowledge of the Father; you share with Him His secrets; are led into Trinitarian life, into the family life of the Godhead.

St. Bonaventure defines faith as "a habit of the mind whereby we are drawn and captivated into the following of Christ." Faith as it grows, according to the Saint, means much more than a cold assent of the mind to dogmas, and articles of faith. It means more than the fulfillment of duties and obligations. It is, rather, the response of a whole man, a total commitment to a Person, a way of life; and always, at its deepest, most real level, a personal encounter with a living God.

Faith must grow. If not, man stagnates, becomes a religious moron. How does it grow? By exercising the power of faith, throwing it into action. And how is that done? There are three principal ways:

1. *Thinking* about God and divine things. Seeing everything against the background of eternity. Seeing through people, things, events into the will and love and plan of God. Seeing Christ in everyone.

2. *Reading*. A daily program of good spiritual reading, especially the *Life of Christ*.
3. *Prayer*. Living in the constant *awareness* of God. Practicing, until it becomes a habit, the presence of God. Cultivating a consciousness of the Trinity in the soul. Spending some time every day in intimate, personal, solitary communion with God.

VII

Love. When your love of God is perfect you are perfect. That's how simple the spiritual life is. Love is everything. Other things have value to the extent that they cause love, intensify love, or preserve love. Apart from love, humility, penance, and the like, have no meaning.

"At the end of life we will be judged by love. . . . One act of pure love is worth far more than all sorts of all other activities put together." So spoke St. John of the Cross. St. Francis de Sales said that a flick of the finger done with two ounces of love is worth more than martyrdom done with only one ounce of love. So it's not what you do but with how much love you do it.

Charity was infused at baptism. How does it grow so that by great love man is transformed into Christ and given the possession of God and His kingdom? Once again it is by throwing the theological virtue, the supernatural power into action. There are three principal ways:

1. *By loving*. Thinking, hearing, studying about God is not enough. Your love of God can grow only by loving Him. You cannot learn to swim or drive by reading a book on swimming or driving; you've got to exercise the skill — what little you might have — until it becomes a habit. So it is with loving God. You don't have to feel it or thrill to it, it is chiefly an act of will.

You are not meant to love only God, but to love everyone and everything in God. You grow in love by loving God's creation, God's world, God's people. And so you must be full of concern and respect for all God's creatures. You are responsible for the whole world.

2. *By doing everything out of love.* Every item and aspect of your life must be offered to God out of love or it is wasted. God doesn't want some of your life, some of the time; He wants the whole man all of the time. All that you do should, therefore, be motivated, permeated, and crowned by love. Then *all* of your human life sanctifies you.

3. *Sacrifice* has always been and always will be the greatest proof of love. What is sacrifice? A preference of one thing over another. A loaf of bread is preferred to a quarter; and so the quarter is sacrificed. God is preferred to everything and so everything that would vie and compete with God, that would distract man's mind or divide his heart is sacrificed. That's what our Lord meant when He said: "Trade till I come."

APPENDIX I

Outline of Retreat Preparation

The following is a bare outline of an excellent form of preparation used yearly with unusually good effect by Father Richard Tormey, Chaplain, and the Sisters of Mercy at Our Lady of Mercy High School, Rochester, New York.

Enclosure No. 1

February 24, 1960

Dear Parents:

On Wednesday morning your daughter begins a three-day Retreat at school. To help her gain its richest benefits we have brought two excellent Retreat Masters to Mercy and have made elaborate arrangements of schedule involving four conferences a day, Mass and Holy Communion, opportunities for confession, time for private prayer and meditation.

May I respectfully suggest a few ways in which you might help maintain the retreat atmosphere in your home on Wednesday and Thursday evenings.

The girls will spend the Retreat Day in silence but this is not expected nor even desired at home. However, it would help the "carry-over" of her spirit of Retreat if she would give up her TV viewing, radio listening, and record playing for these two evenings. Please suggest in their place that she continue the spiritual reading she has been doing during the day at school. Urge an earlier bedtime for her.

Having a daughter on Retreat should not bring sacrifices on the family, so I'm not suggesting that you turn off the

TV or radio. Merely sidetrack daughter from them to a quieter room.

Dating, or going out to other girls' homes or to the movies or for skating or for a ride will also break the Retreat mood of Wednesday and Thursday. We are asking the girls to make a two-evening sacrifice of all these pleasures. Please help her make the decision to pass them up so as to come to school next day not too far removed from the Retreat spirit.

The telephone, too, should not be ringing much in Mercy homes this week if each Mercian decides not to break in on her friends' Retreat by the usual calls. Such a two-evening voluntary boycott of the phone may alarm the Rochester Telephone Corporation, but it would be a helpful mortification.

I hope your daughter's Retreat prayers and graces gained will bless your whole family. May you note with proud satisfaction that these days have helped her grow more mature and clear-headed and noble-souled.

Respectfully in Our Lady,
RICHARD TORMEY
Chaplain

A. Retreat preparation at Our Lady of Mercy begins with open discussion at Student-Faculty Forum exactly three weeks before the Retreat. (Some 25 students and 10 faculty members attend.)

The chaplain reviews schedule and activities of the year before, sketches new ideas for spirit and asks for comment on last year's Retreat. Student officers contribute imaginatively to this planning and later convey details to their home rooms. They are recognized by students as coiners of phrases and slogans used and instigators of some of disciplinary measures for Retreat order.

B. Prayer preparation in school days immediately preceding Wednesday opening of Retreat:

    Five days (Wednesday, Thursday, Friday, Monday, Tuesday) of Masses at school and home-room prayers for Retreat success on "hard souls"; five days of visits to the Blessed Sacrament and daily Rosary for "particular targets" (students). These are voluntary but remarkably well attended.

C. The chaplain gives first Pre-Retreat Conference to whole school on Friday preceding Wednesday opening of Retreat:

    a) Purposes of Retreat: self-examination, guidance, graces, careers, etc.

    b) General treatment of plans: schedule, silence, reading, thinking, sacraments.

    c) Emphasis on good confession and good resolutions for all.

    d) Prayer for those who need sacraments most.

    e) Make good confession this week end before opening of Retreat, for gaining state of grace.

    f) Plan Retreat confession to seek advice, discuss major weaknesses, solve "problems."

D. A week before Retreat:

    The chaplain writes letter to home of every student (Enclosure No. 1) suggesting ways parents could help girls keep Retreat spirit on the two evenings of Retreat.

E. A week before Retreat:

    Sophomore representatives visit all freshman home rooms to indoctrinate freshmen on "what is a retreat?" A few days later two Seniors visit same home rooms to help Freshmen get right mental start.

F. The library publicizes Retreat books and pamphlets available and invites students to make good selection on the two days before Retreat.

G. On the two school days immediately before Retreat:

The chaplain and four local parish priests hear confessions 10:30 to noon and 1 p.m. to 3 p.m. (We have strong feeling that putting as many as possible in state of grace *before* Retreat opens brings richer Retreat graces.)

H. The day before Retreat, the Office publishes a bulletin for each girl to keep, listing rules and schedule and suggestions for Retreat activity.

I. The day before Retreat, the school paper publishes special "Retreat Issue" containing articles and pictures to heighten retreat spirit.

J. The day before Retreat, the chaplain gives inspirational second Pre-Retreat conference covering purposes of Retreat, means of making it well, goals to seek.

Covering the theme "Walk Alone With God" he plays up slogans: "Abandon Your Pals"; "Eat With Strangers"; "Keep Your Mind Open for God Alone to Talk to You."

K. On the opening morning of Retreat, silence begins when girls alight from buses to enter school. (Slogan for three days: "Silence from bus door to bus door.")

L. On arrival in home room on first day of Retreat, each girl pins on a ribbon (in the proper class colors) lettered "Walk Alone With God" to serve as silence reminder for herself and others during three days.

M. On arrival in home room, each girl is asked to sign voluntarily and keep till final afternoon a "Silence Pledge." This had been explained in home room earlier with full interpretation on what constituted "breaking the pledge." On last afternoon, girls voluntarily countersigned pledge if they had kept silence for three days and deposited pledge in their proper class box before the altar as gift from her class. (Must emphasize voluntary element and being honest toward God.)

N. Schedule.

Freshmen and Sophomores have Mass, Conferences, Benedictions, and visits in the gymnasium where portable altar, communion rails, portable organ, etc., have been arranged to transform place into a chapel.

Juniors and Seniors have all their exercises in the Auditorium.

Schedule is staggered to minimize traffic conflicts in corridors: students' activities are quieter and less distracting if the two lower classes rarely see or meet the upper classes. Scheduling one program some 5 minutes or so ahead of the other permits the chaplain to assist both Retreat Masters in distributing Holy Communion at Mass and helps maintain quiet decorum at dismissal time each afternoon.

O. On all cafeteria tables there are little brackets holding a "silence intention." These were rotated after each meal to offer new reminders of why to make sacrifice of not speaking at meals. (Samples: "For the intentions of the Holy Father," "For the missionaries in India," "For the soldiers in Korea," "For the teen-agers behind the Iron Curtain.")

P. Pamphlet supplies (free loan) and books for spiritual reading are available to all at a half dozen alcoves around the school and on table in each home room.

Q. Each individual home-room teacher plans program to occupy girls when not in a conference. Long period (including lunch time) from end of the second morning conference and beginning of afternoon conference, is filled in most home rooms by Sister directing Rosary, Examination of Conscience, and spiritual reading. Girls who wanted to do all this by themselves were permitted to do so, in Chapel.

R. Daily Confession facilities:

Both Retreat Masters and chaplain hear confessions

for about 20 minutes before Mass on 2nd and 3rd Retreat mornings; and for about 30–60 minutes after the afternoon Benedictions; and in between the morning and afternoon conferences of all three days.

Six diocesan priests come on second and third days of Retreat to hear confessions from 11:45 to 1:15.

S. We use a "number system" for the confessional lines: when the priest must leave the confessional the first 10 students still left in the line pick up a small cardboard number from 1 to 10 from a box beside the confessional. The next time that confessor returns to the confessional the students holding tickets return the numbers to the box and take their former place in the line according to the number they held. This system assures each girl a fair chance at getting to the confessor of her choice with only a normal amount of waiting time and no racing to the confessional or jockeying for position.

T. On the final afternoon after the second P.M. conference, Freshmen and Sophomores move from gymnasium to auditorium for Benediction and Papal Blessing. We usually are honored by the presence of our Most Reverend Ordinary who gives brief talk and presides at this final Benediction of Blessed Sacrament for the whole student body.

U. The Journalism Class takes notes at all conferences by both Retreat Masters and publishes each day for distribution to each student a "Rehash" or review of the pertinent points of the conferences. This daily mimeographed one-sheet newspaper also contains announcements of schedule, confessors, points of Retreat discipline, etc., thus reducing to a minimum the necessity of using the school public-address system during the Retreat.

V. On the first day of Retreat each girl receives a small

school-produced notebook with the hymns to be sung before the conferences, at the Masses and Benedictions, and three or four blank pages for note-taking.

W. The Art Department prepares in advance of Retreat a collection of fifty to seventy-five posters and Retreat reminders. These are hung in corridors, lavatories, locker room areas, wherever the girls might need a visual stimulant to stay in the Retreat mood at all times. At the end of the first and the second days of the Retreat the entire display is shifted to new locations around the school. We find that this form of pictorial propaganda, because of the slogans or ideas that the posters contain, constitutes a continuous reminder to each student of the purposes and goals of the Retreat.

X. The Mission Unit of the student body prepares in advance of the Retreat a series of projects for student busy-work when the girls are in the home rooms and not actually engaged in reading or thinking or prayer. Projects: rolling bandages, repairing used rosaries, assembling mounted holy cards and religious pictures for mission school use, small sewing projects of clothing that will be sent to mission schools, etc. These fill in free time for those students who find that they get restless and bored between conferences, or when their reading or silence grows dull. Projects, of course, are done under the guidance of the home-room teacher and in total silence.

APPENDIX II

Christopher Tips: Prepare Now for the Future

Make the most of these years of your teens. Lay foundations that are deep and solid. If you do, you will build for time and eternity. Here are a few tips which may prove helpful:

SUGGESTION 1 — MAKE YOUR LIFE GOD-CENTERED

If you wish to be a man or woman of strong character, develop the powers of mind, heart, and soul that God has entrusted to you. To be outwardly forceful, you must be inwardly strong. Live by principle, not by emotion or expediency.

Center your life in God. See in the Church His divine instrument to guide, instruct, and fortify you. Cultivate the habit of daily spiritual exercises. Be conscientious about such practices as morning and evening prayers, examination of conscience, grace at meals, a brief reading from the New Testament and some spiritual books. The repetition of these will keep you mindful that you are always in the presence of God and will gradually build up an inner power that you could obtain in no other way.

SUGGESTION 2 — RESPECT AUTHORITY

It is a human weakness to avoid obligations and responsibilities. But a boy who wants to be a good football player knows that he has to respect authority and live up to the rules of training.

Anyone who wants to further what is good and decent in a modern world must have more than superficial roots. He should be grounded in that truth of which God alone is the Author.

No Angel comes down from heaven to tell each of us what to do. God has chosen to delegate part of His authority to others.

All true authority of parents, religious, teachers, civic officials and others in similar positions of responsibility has its origin in the Almighty.

There is nothing new about this. 1900 years ago Paul the Apostle reminded the Christians of Rome that they should obey the reigning authorities in everything that was truly lawful. Here is the way he put it: *"Let everyone submit himself to the ruling authorities, for there exists no authority not ordained by God. And that which exists has been constituted by God. Therefore he who opposes such authority resists the ordinance of God, and they that resist bring condemnation on themselves"* (Rom. 13:1–3).

In co-operating with those in authority, then, see God's hand in every just direction. Therefore, obey (a) willingly, (b) cheerfully, (c) quickly, and (d) completely.

SUGGESTION 3 — RESTORE THE FAMILY CIRCLE

In our busy, distracted world, many things can interfere with normal life. But this need not be. As a teen-ager, you can lead the way in restoring the "togetherness" of your family. While others talk about the "breakdown" of the home, do something to "build up" and strengthen the foundations of true family life.

The good family is the very basis of a good nation. A country becomes weak when family life is neglected. Popularize the idea of what one teen-ager can do to correct a dangerous trend in our country. Practices such as the following can help:

a) *Dine Together* — Promote the custom of all members of the family eating at least one meal a day together. Make it a happy and important ceremony of home life, an occasion to share ideas and experiences.

b) *Time With Parents* — Spend time with your parents. Set aside a regular time each day, however brief, to be with them. You can learn much from them and they can learn from you! A wise and kindly old man, when asked how he acquired his unusual qualities, replied quite simply: "When I was young, I made it a point to spend part of my time with older people. As I got old myself, I made it my business to spend time with young people."

c) *Brothers and Sisters* — Be loyal to your brothers and sisters. Take time to be in their company, to discuss problems with them, to work and play with them.

d) *Pray Together* — Protect the sacred side of home life by encouraging, as already touched upon, regular attendance at Church, family prayers, reading of the Bible, and saying grace at meals together.

e) *First Things First* — A recent poll of 180,000 senior high school girls conducted by General Mills revealed that 83 per cent were well informed in the art of keeping themselves "neat and pretty"; 71 per cent had studied up on how to "keep a husband happy"; 64 per cent had a good knowledge of the mechanics of housekeeping, but only 52 per cent had acquired "real cooking skills."

Help remedy this dangerous trend by encouraging teenage girls to prepare for the lifelong vocation and honor of being a good homemaker — for the domestic, spiritual, and cultural role that she is privileged to play as a wife and mother.

SUGGESTION 4 — UPHOLD THE SANCTITY
OF THE BODY

Whenever atheistic totalitarians start to undermine a country, a top "must" on their program is to instill in young people the idea that they are nothing but animals. They know from experience that through education, literature, films, recordings, etc., they can stir up the lowest instincts in teen-agers and that eventually more than a few of them will act like animals.

You can prevent and change this degrading policy by emphasizing the sanctity of the human being, both body and soul.

One of the best reminders of the holiness of man is St. Paul's stern warning to the corrupt Corinthians: "Do you not know that you are God's temple and that God's spirit dwells in you? If anyone destroys God's temple, God will destroy you, for God's temple, which you yourselves are, is holy" (1 Cor. 3:16–17).

Get busy without delay in spreading such points as these:

a) *Partners In Creation* — God has entrusted to you a bit of His power of creation. One day as a father or mother you may help to give life to a new human being — a precious body and soul. In His generosity to all who assume the great responsibility of parenthood, God provides a special pleasure for those who are partners with Him in this sacred undertaking. But He insists that this pleasure be conscientiously reserved to the holy state of marriage, not abused outside of it.

b) *Respect Your Privilege* — Show your appreciation for the honor of being a future father or mother by treating your body — and those of others — with a holy respect.

c) *Master It Always* — Learn early to be the master of your physical impulses, not the slave. God has entrusted a tremendous power to you. He leaves it to you to control it. Mistakes in this important matter can plague you for the rest of your life and rob you of your peace of soul for time and eternity. Resist the beginnings of temptations and you will save yourself much trouble.

d) *Uphold Decency* — You can be a vital force in refreshing and elevating the tone of television, movies, music, magazines, comics and similar outlets if you make it a practice to encourage those which uphold the sanctity of the human being. You can likewise discourage the spread of what is immoral, cheap, or brutal by withdrawing your support from all presentations which feature what is low and vulgar. Protect your right of choice and stir up adults as well as teen-agers to uphold decency.

SUGGESTION 5 — SET YOUR SIGHTS HIGH

Many young people develop the habit of just "drifting" through their teens. As a result, they often go through a whole lifetime without ever discovering the bit of greatness within them.

You can have a hand in shaping the future if you make it your business while in high school, to develop and channel your God-given talent toward a big and worthwhile objective. Keep in mind:

a) that you have only one life to live;

b) that the world itself will be a little better or a little worse because you have been in it;

c) that your life will take on new meaning and purpose once you realize that God has given you a particular mission in life to perform — one that He has assigned to no one else;

d) that by trying to be a Christopher or Christ-bearer on every occasion, you can experience the deep satisfaction of being a personal ambassador of almighty God Himself;

e) that by taking up a career in a field that counts, you can help shape the lives of millions and thus do more than merely earn a living for yourself.

If enough teen-agers like you with Christlike purpose and ability would take up careers in government, education, labor relations and entertainment, you would play a vital role in shaping the world of tomorrow.

INDEX